Contents

Chapter 1--------------------Introduction

Chapter 2--------------------Immigration

Chapter 3--------------------Racism

Chapter 4 -------------------Terrorism

Chapter 5 -------------------Armed Conflict

Chapter 1
Introduction

International Law:-

        International law commonly referred to as "Public International Law " regulates the relations and activities between nations. It also contains rules and regulations regarding the operation of International organizations, such as the United Nations. In addition it governs state treatment of individuals and juridical persons(i.e non natural persons such as corporations, association or partnership).

International law is distinct from private international law(Conflict of laws) which regulates dealings between individual and juridical persons from different states.

According to Prof. L. Oppenheim International law is " The law of nations or international law is the name for the body of customary and conventional rules which are considered legally binding by civilised states in their intercourse with each other".

International law refers to nations as sovereign states. In this context sovereign states does not mean states within a nations. Furthermore in USA and India individual states lack authority to engage in international dealings. The constitutions of these countries explicitly denies states this power, and vests it with the federal government.

International law encompasses several areas, such as international trade, the creation and dissolution of states, use of force(regarding when a state may initiate force against another state), armed conflict("humanitarian law " regarding how a state conducts an armed conflict), Human Rights (as given Universal declaration of Human Rights), refugees, crimes, environment , labor, the sea, air space & postal services.

Sources of International Law

According to Article 38 of the statute of International Court of Justice, following is the order of the use of sources of International Law:

(1) International Conventions,
(2) International Customs,
(3) General principles of law recognized by civilized nations,
(4) Judicial decisions and juristic opinion as

subsidiary means for the determination of rules of International Law

International Law and Municipal Law

It is a well settled law that municipal laws have to be in conformity with the International Law.

The following are the main theories governing the relations of municipal laws and International Law

(1) **Monism:**

According to this theory law is a unified field of knowledge, no matter whether it applies on individuals, states or other entities.

(2) **Dualism:**

This theory says that International Law and municipal law are two different laws. It says that an individual is the subject of state law whereas state is the subject of international law. The origin of state law is the will of state whereas origin of international law is the common will of the states

I. The Concept of "Constitution"

The concept of "constitution" has no precise meaning fixed once and **for** all. Generally, constitution is a term employed with regard to national legal systems only,[1] while international mechanisms within which States cooperate have rarely been identified **by** that word. In its recent jurisprudence, the Court of Justice of the European Communities has furthermore used the label of constitution in characterizing the basic treaties on which those Communities and the European Union overarching them are founded.[2] Notwithstanding its proximity to the State or to entities developing para-statal characteristics, however, the concept of constitution has or can be given a much broader meaning, in accordance with

current linguistic usages.
It may be taken to designate the basic legal framework of a given human community, its essential structures and the ties which hold it together.
To be sure, as long as the relevant rules have not been formally defined as such, one may have different views as to what belongs to that hard core. Yet reflection permits to specify at least *grosso modo* the different components which, in their combination, make up a constitution.
It is a truism to state that the main task of any constitution is to enable human beings to live peacefully together in such a way that both the existence of the community concerned as well as the lives of its members are protected. Constitutions serve to establish a viable

' In the words of Dicey. constitutional law includes "alrlul es which directly or indirectly affect the distribution or the exercise of the sovereign power in the State", **A.** V. Dicey. *Introduction to the Study of the Law of the Constitution,*

overcome. This presupposes that there exist ground rules determining
and allocating the main functions which must be discharged in order
to keep a political system on good course. These functions are, with
slight variations, the same for every human community. In the first
place, human beings need common rules which reconcile the freedom
of everyone with everyone else's freedom. In balancing these mutual
claims, the art consists in keeping necessary sacrifices to a minimum.
Freedom for all under conditions of equality must not degenerate into
freedom for nobody. Be that as it may, it is not the detailed outcome
of such regulatory processes which forms part of a constitution but

rather the rule that confers on a specific body the power to enact provisions binding on everyone.4 Second, it stands to reason that any rules enacted require to be enforced **by** some executive agency.

Lastly, if peace is to be kept within a given group, there must be mechanisms that permit the members of the group to settle their disputes in an orderly and peaceful manner. Again, the rules identifying the institutions entrusted with law enforcement or settlement of legal disputes have a logical priority over others that may arise from carrying out the different activities. They can certainly be counted among the central components of a constitution. The question of who is entitled to exercise the relevant powers is the key issue in any system of governance.

Naturally, a constitution deserves its name only

if its rules are being effectively observed and enforced. **If** it is reduced to a purely rhetorical claim without any correspondence in life, it may at most be called a nominal constitution.5 Under such circumstances, however, the term loses its value as an analytical tool suitable to better understand political realities. **A** constitution, in order truly to deserve its name, must be an effective constitution.6 Its words must be a true reflection of the prevailing way and manner in which public powers are exercised within a given society.

II. The Need for an International Constitution

1. The question may be asked whether mankind does indeed need a constitution in the sense just described. Robinson, having become the

force is its effectiveness.

sole inhabitant of a remote island, could lead an autonomous, self-sufficient existence. Still today, there may be some indigenous groups living in the middle of the jungle without any contact with the outside world. Generally, however, the situation has changed dramatically since international law in the modern sense came into being in the middle of the seventeenth century. At that time-and even before- Europe was a continent torn by rivalries and wars not only between close neighbours, but pitting the most diverse coalitions against each other. In other continents, similar developments took place. But the different theatres of events were in most instances well separated from one another. Occurrences in Asia or Africa did not have immediate repercussions on other continents, the main connecting element being the fight for supremacy between the colonial powers of Europe.

Even as late as the second half of the nineteenth century, the world had not really become a universal whole. Large stretches in Africa and Asia had not yet joined the mainstream of intercourse among nations, but continued their disconnected existence outside the rapidly developing world of modern technology and communication.

Since the creation of the United Nations in 1945, for the first time in the history of mankind a worldwide network of interaction has gradually come into being. While in earlier centuries the different communities had relatively few mutual contacts, except %kithth eir immediate neighbours, today a vast array of factors can be indicated that *de facto* tie all the nations of the globe together. Any major development in one country will therefore cause repercussions somewhere else, and not only just across the next border. A classical link is constituted by international trade, and yet the mutual interrelated nature of the world economy has advanced at such a fast pace and reached such dimensions that today any crisis in one of the leading economies of the world affects all other economies within days or weeks only.

But the most dramatic changes have occurred with regard to the factors determining not only the natural habitat of man, but nature as a whole. Air and water cannot be imprisoned behind national boundary pillars; they move freely from land to sea or around the globe and take with them on their course any contamination they may have suffered by human activity. As a result of all the deleterious effects produced by modern industrialized societies, even the climate of this globe has come under serious threat of profound-and unwelcome-changes; similarly, the progressive destruction of the ozone layer is the result of activities undertaken in all parts of the world. Lastly, the phenomenon of human migration should be referred to. Invariably, policies of repression by dictatorial power wielders, ethnic wars or patterns of poverty and famine trigger flows of human beings, only some of them being refugees in a formal sense, who seek safe havens in other countries, frequently far away from their countries of origin. Thus, even in a region like Western Europe that has enjoyed peace for more than five decades and may continue to do so under a commonly established system of close cooperation, there is no reason for boundless

optimism since many of the factors mentioned may affect the future
in an unforeseen manner. Goethe's comment that every bourgeois
leans comfortably back when being apprised of battles between peoples
"far away in Turkey"[7] has definitely been overtaken by events.
Today, any news about social tension and armed conflict somewhere
in the world, irrespective of their location, must ring an alarm bell
precisely in nations living under conditions of peace because, more
than any other nations, they are vitally dependent on the continuance
of that favourable state of affairs.

2. It may seem a Herculean task to see all this- and many more
problems-tackled by the international community. And yet to face
up to the tasks transcending national boundaries is inevitable. Mankind
does need a stable framework for action that at

least seeks to deal with the existing and any newly emerging problems in a fair and equitable manner. For that purpose, clear-cut premises are needed.

Mankind should be prepared to face up to the challenges confronting it in a spirit of rationality by peaceful means, respecting the rights of all of its members. Of course, one could also embrace a more cynical approach, referring to the famous dictum that "war is the father of all things" (Heraclit). But if war is left to shape the destiny of mankind, this amounts to opening the gates of anarchy and death. What is needed is a reliable foundation for the life of future generations. *Aprس nous le diluge* has never been the motto of a political constitution supported by a people as a whole. It may be the leitmotif of a group in a society that realizes that its time has run out. If ever an attempt is made to pave the way into the future in a responsible way, the principles of peace and justice must indicate the general direction.

3. It is clear that a universal framework for action, a constitution of mankind, cannot be directly related to the individual human being. No system seeking to regulate the interaction among more than 5 billion persons would be viable. Rather, the existing power centres have to be relied upon by necessity. States do exist as entities which peoples generally view as the legitimate expression of their political aspirations and within which they are able to develop a true sense of solidarity-something which at the universal level is also proclaimed, but remains a somewhat artificial construction. They are able to bundle and focus all the energies and forces of their

citizens, and therefore they constitute indispensable building blocks when it comes to establishing any kind of legal framework at a higher level. This does not detract from the fact that the human being remains the final beneficiary of the entire system of international law. But the individual cannot be given a decisive role within the mechanisms of a world constitution. The sheer weight of numbers makes it necessary to rely on representative institutions. In this sense, every State and every Government play the role of a representative of its people.

THE LAW OF THE INTERNATIONAL COMMUNITY

According to jurist **Igor Ivanovich Lukashuk** Mankind is approaching a historic turning-point: the beginning of the third millennium of the common era. Today there is an especially

keen desire to look into the future and try to see what it holds. It is
therefore quite natural that more and more new works on the subject
of the future, including the future of international law, are being published.

On the eve of the twenty-first century, highly significant events
are taking place in the field of international law. The United Nations
has celebrated its first half-century. The International Law Commission
is now approaching its fiftieth anniversary. These dates fall
during the United Nations Decade of International Law, which closes
the twentieth century. These events are not as fortuitous as they may
seem. They point to the fact that the coming century will be one of an
international community truly based on law, a century of universal
rule of law. International law will become the

law of the international community.

In recent years, the expression "international community" has become firmly established not only in political instruments but also in legal instruments. It is also finding its way into the domestic law of individual States. Thus, there is a provision in the Preamble of the Constitution of the Russian Federation in accordance with which the People adopted the Constitution "recognizing [itself] as a part of the world community".[2] This is a reflection of a new, contemporary relation to the surrounding world based on the notion of an organic link to the world community. Russia, as any other country, cannot pursue

'There are quite a few publications of this kind, such as R. J. Dupuy, ed., *The Future of international Law in a Multicultural World*

2 The expression "world community" is usually used to denote two concepts.
In one instance it means the same thing as "international community-; in another.
it may be defined as the "community of peoples" or "mankind".
its national interests in isolation but only in cooperation with other
countries as a member of the international community.
Contemporary international law, often called post-confronta.
tional, constitutes a revival of the law of the Charter of the United
Nations. This historic document reflected the hopes and dreams of
mankind, which had endured untold suffering during the Second
World War. At the time, even conservative statesmen could not ignore
such aspirations. To a large extent, the Cold War halted the process of
restructuring international law and international relations on the basis

of the purposes and principles of the Charter. However, one cannot fail to observe that, notwithstanding the icy armour of the Cold War, international law continued to develop. This bears witness to the vitality of the process of the progressive development of international law. We must emphasize the role that the International Law Commission played in this process. While the purposes and principles of the Charter were to a considerable extent only formally recognized during the Cold War, they are now becoming part of the daily practice of international relations and serve as the basis for restructuring international law. Postconfrontational international law is creating the preconditions for the transition to the law of the international community.

Since the adoption of the Charter of the United Nations, the

world has changed significantly, attaining a new degree of unity as a
result of strengthened ties between States and their greater interdependence.
Today, new ways must be found to solve the fundamental
foreign policy problem faced by States, namely, the problem of
striking a balance between national and international interests.
Achieving such optimal balance depends to a great extent on international
law. Indeed, that is one of its most important functions especially
in the present-day world.
Today, international law should be based on the concept of an
international community. This approach should be followed by all
nations so as to further the goals of promoting peace, security and
global economic, scientific and technological development and of
establishing a modern method of regulation of

the world system, as well as to make effective use of international law. It is only if mankind manages to develop a united community that it will be able to fight successfully for its own survival.[3]

[3] See the following statement by V. Petrovsky: "The recognition of the unity of the world and its interdependence is the main focal point in the process of transition of the international community to the new world system of peace, cooperation and security based on the United Nations Charter". V. Petrovsky. "Disarmament and National Security in an Interdependent World". *Disarmament Topical Papers 16* (United Nations publication, Sales No. E.94.IX.3), p. 19.

One of the reasons for the difficulties currently experienced by the international community is that great and small Powers alike do not recognize their collective and individual responsibilities to buttress

the world order.' Russia's position on this issue was stated by
President Yeltsin in the following manner:
"Any country, whether large or small, should be aware of its
responsibilities for maintenance of order based on law and morality...
only a profound understanding on the part of each participant
in international cooperation, of his or her individual
responsibility can engender a common sense of responsibility for
the world situation." [5]

The new world order and corresponding law should have a firm moral
basis and should promote social justice. It will be the order and law
of the international community.

present
-or cultural-arising from a plurality of peoples

with their own histories, traditions and beliefs. It is evident also in the domain of law, despite the unifying influences of the major legal traditions. 2

At the level of international relations, diversity is perhaps less pronounced. The reasons for this include the limited number of actors (States, public international organizations, even international nongovernmental organizations with a significant profile), the tendency for a smaller number of actors still to set the major agendas for debate and the use of a more or less common set of ideas.3 One might add, too, the socializing tendency of intergovernmental diplomacy, and, more fundamentally, the complex, diffuse but undeniable effects of "globalization" which has accentuated the trend towards relative uniformity in recent years.4

Nonetheless even at the international level there have always
been significant divergences of policy, interest and approach amongst
States and groups of States. The historic divisions between nations in
the modern period (colonizers and colonized, socialist and non-socialist,
first and third world, aligned and non-aligned, developed and developing)
have had their effects. Those divisions have been accompanied
at various times by such ideological outriders as the distinction
between "civilized" and "'uncivilized" nations,5 the idea of "socialist"
chapter are on the whole independent of the answer one gives to the historical question.

2 The effect of those traditions in *entrenching* distinctive underlying attitudes
and modes of legal reasoning has also been emphasized. See P. Legrand, "European
Legal Systems Are Not Converging". *ICLQ*. vol.

45 (1996). p. 52.
1 On the common "stock of concepts", see I. Brownlic, "The Expansion of International Society: The Consequences for the Law of Nations", in H. Bull and

The distinction had some currency in the later nineteenth century: see. e.g.,
J. Hornung, "Civilisds et Barbares", *Revue de droit international et de ligislation comparde,* vol. 17 **(1885),** pp. 5-18,447-470 and 539-560; *ibid,* vol. 18 (1886), pp. **188-**206 and 281-298. It has been argued that in *some* form it is even necessary today.
See **G.** W. Gong, *The Standard of Civilization in International Society* (Oxford, Clarendon Press, 1984). It is echoed, of course, in the reference to "civilized nations" in article 38, paragraph I *(c),* of the Statute of the International Court (itself repeated by the International Law Commission in the 1958 Model Rules on Arbitral Procedure, article 10). In the *Western Sahara* case the Court itself plainly

rejected "civilization". in preference to "social organization", as a criterion for the capacity of a society to hold rights over territory. *LC.J. Reports 1975,* p. 12.
international law,6 and the claim to a special status for the international law of decolonization and of development.7 Alongside struggles at a more or less "global" level by reference to these and other polarities, there has been a continuous development of special, and especially regional, approaches and institutions.

This reflects the fact that although the situation of every State or nation may be attributed to its "'place in the world", that "place" tends first of all to be seen in terms of its immediate neighbours and its own region. Moreover in many cases the things which Governments and officials spend most time on, and which they can do most to affect, tend to be issues relating to neighbours or to the region. Even when the focus is on matters of apparently universal concern, the approach of many Governments is likely to be profoundly affected by regional postures and implications-and not only in such contexts as minority rights or the non-navigational uses of international watercourses. Thus, in addition to earlier claims to "regional international law" in the Americas,' the period since 1945 has seen the active and often vigorous development of regional approaches to peace and security,

There has been a significant regional involvement in some "peace-keeping" issues (e.g., Liberia, Haiti), and the European Community asserted priority of concern at various stages of the Yugoslav crisis.

resources, 2 the settlement of disputes,3

disarmament (especially in the nuclear field),[4] and of course economic development and free trade.[5]

One cannot but stress also the underlying economic differences between countries and regions, the problems of continued underdevelopment, especially in Africa and parts of Asia,[6] of internal armed conflict and associated displacement of persons,[7] and of the influence of different religious beliefs. The underlying diversity of nations and the tendency to regionalism even in respect of areas, such as human rights, where universal values would appear to be at stake, raises significant tensions for international law and may even call in question its claim to "universality".[8]

Chapter 2

Immigration

Immigration seems to be making more headlines in recent years. As the world globalizes in terms of nations' economies, trade and investment, borders are opened up more easily for "freer" flow of goods and products. People are supposedly freer to move around the world, too.

Introduction—Worldwide Immigrants Statistics

- Worldwide, there is an estimated 191 million immigrants;
- The last 50 years has seen an almost doubling of immigration;
- 115 million immigrants live in developed countries;
- 20% (approximately 38 million) live in the

US alone, making up 13% of its population;
- 33% of all immigrants live in Europe;
- 75% live in just 28 countries;
- Women constitute approximately half of all migrants at around 95 million;
- Between 1990 and 2005
  - There were 36 million migrations (an average of approximately 2.4 million per year);
  - 33 million wound up in industrialized countries;
  - 75% of the increases occurred in just 17 countries;
  - Immigration decreased in 72 countries in the same period;

Why Do People Emigrate?

People emigrate from one country to another for a variety of complex reasons. Some are forced to move, due to conflict or to escape persecution and prejudices, while others may voluntarily emigrate. Although such a move may be necessary, it can be quite traumatic on top of the challenges experienced so far.

From another perspective, immigration can also represent an act of courage. For example,

- Moving to a different country with different culture and norms can be quite daunting;
- The potential loneliness to be suffered is not always easy to overcome;
- There may be the additional pressure to earn enough to live (in a more expensive-to-live-in country) *and* send back meager savings.

An economic migrant, a person searching for work, or better opportunities, will be stepping into the unknown—an exciting prospect if the person is already well-to-do, or daunting at least, if out of desperation.

As *Inter Press Service* (IPS) reported, the European Union has recently acknowledged a concern about immigration that has not received much media attention. That is, <u>a large number of people are attempting to leave the devastation of their own country caused by the</u>

<u>current form of globalization</u> and other political and economic policies, which, as well as creating winners, is creating a large number of losers, and increasing inequality. Tackling poverty and addressing issues of development and opportunity are important aspects of tackling this type of immigration.

Effects of Immigration

Immigration can have positive and negative impacts on both the host (recipient) country, and the original country.

The recipient country is usually an industrialized country in Western Europe, or the United States. For these countries, immigrants offer various benefits such as the following:

- Immigrants will often do jobs that people in the host country will not, or cannot do;
- Migrant workers often work longer hours and for lower salaries, and while that is controversial, sometimes exploitive, it benefits the host country;
- Immigrants, when made to feel welcome in the host society, can contribute to the diversity of that society, which can help with

tolerance and understanding;
- For the host country's economy, immigrants offer an increased talent pool, if they have been well educated in their original country.

But there are also numerous drawbacks:

- Immigrants can be exploited for their cheap labor;
- Developing countries may suffer "brain drain" as the limited resources they spend in educating their students amount to very little if that talent is enticed to another country. (The UK for example is often accused of actively hiring medical staff from developing countries. The previous link details this issue further.)
- Immigration can also attract criminal elements, from trafficking in drugs and people to other forms of crime and corruption;
- Immigration can become a social/political issue, where racism can be used to exploit feelings or as an excuse for current woes of local population;
- Where there is a perception that immigrants and refugees appear to get more benefits than local poor people, tensions and

hostilities can also rise;
- Concerns about illegal immigration can spill over to ill-feelings towards the majority of immigrants who are law-abiding and contributing to the economy;
- Many die trying to flee their predicament, and this can often make sensational headlines giving the appearance that immigration is largely illegal and "out of control."

Despite what appears to be large population movements, Gary Younge, from the *Guardian* noted some time ago that people still are not able to move as freely as commodities. In some places around the world, there are additional restrictions being put up on people's movements.

United States

New York-based *Human Rights Watch* reports on how the US Immigration and Naturalization Service treat immigration detainees as though they were criminals by putting these otherwise innocent people in jail, indefinitely.

US immigration policies, (especially noticeable during the economic boom at the end of the 1990s) are interesting in that they are really designed to bring in immigrants with a certain level and type of education to help enhance the nation, economically. While at first thought this seems reasonable, there are a few ramifications:

- A disproportionate representation of that ethnic population becomes part of the American culture;
- As a result it affects the stereotypical image of such minorities seemingly in a positive way as always being hard-working but also as only interested in the pursuit of financial gains, for example.
- However, a strange twist occurs:
  - Some politicians use such stereotyped groups to show how other immigrant populations in the US who have been around longer should follow newer immigrant's examples
  - Some even using that as a basis to

argue for a further cut in social welfare subsidies for example, unfairly blaming such people solely for their economic problems.

- So, as an unfortunate example, South Asian Americans are inadvertently looked upon negatively by many in the Black and Latino communities, and vice versa.

For more details on this aspect, see for example, Vijay Prashad's books, *The Karma of Brown Folk* (University of Minesota Press, 2000) and *Everybody was Kung Fu Fighting*, (Beacon Press, 2001).

United Kingdom

In 1998, various human rights groups such as Amnesty International UK, <u>expressed concerns</u> at <u>plans to improve the immigration process</u>.

Fears and concerns cited included the following:

- This plan would allow immigration officers more power than before to detain and increase the number of asylum seekers whose appeals have been refused.

o Having more checks by liaison officers at the ports and airports of the countries that the asylum seekers are leaving would prevent genuine asylum seekers being able to flee their country where human rights violations may be taking place.

Even though the number of people seeking asylum in UK is not as large as some other countries in Europe, Amnesty International, for example, raises the concern that **UK's current process means that the prison-like asylum centers house people who may be waiting up to seven years before their case can be heard**.

It would seem that some of these concerns have come true while the media plays to the hype that politicians raise of immigration being "out of control":

Media Coverage

Media portrayal of immigration and asylum issues was quite mainstream in 2003, for example. However, a look at how three mainstream British papers, the *Daily*

Telegraph,The Guardian and *The Independent*, respectively from the political right, left and center, reveals a common set of problems and similar levels of bias, as Matthew Randall summarizes:

As a rule, UK parliamentary debate on asylum and immigration is both selective and power serving. While the actual demographic and economic effects of immigration on the UK are rarely discussed, the causes of immigration — global inequality, conflict and human rights abuses — are ignored.

Irrespective of party, leading politicians repeatedly highlight issues of exclusion — fears of "invasion", alleged "threats" and actual prejudices — ensuring a very negative image of immigrants despite their statistically small impact on society.... Concerns over crime, disease, terrorism, detention and surveillance are consistently pushed well to the fore.

This lack of balance can be attributed to a number of factors, including the existence of a covert racist ideology and the political expediency of "the race card" — factors that repeatedly compromise the welfare of refugees and immigrants.

Honest consideration of asylum and immigration issues should involve a far more diverse range of topics, reflecting the complexity of contemporary national and global relations. These include issues of nationalism, sovereignty, racism, demography, human rights, arms sales, war, refugee health, economic policy and moral responsibility.

Often asked in England is why "everyone" wants to come to England. Yet, Randall, in the same article also notes that wider context is ignored leading to various skewed perceptions:

Is appropriate coverage given, for example, to

the fact that in 2001 the UK had only 169,370 officially recognized refugees living within its borders compared to Germany's 988,500, Iran's 1.9 million or Pakistan's 2.2 million? Are we made sufficiently aware that during the same year the UK received 71,365 applicants for asylum, granting this status to just 11,180 individuals — 0.02% of the UK population? Or that Pakistan received a single influx of 199,900 Afghan refugees? Or that the ten largest refugee movements in 2001 were, with the exception of Yugoslavia, all made between countries in the Third World?

How many of us learn from our press that UK population growth is slowing down to the extent that it has actually become a cause for concern? How many are aware that a 2002 UN report recommended "replacement immigration" as a solution to this problem, or that the recommendation was rejected by the European Commission on the grounds that the impact of immigration on population was insignificant?

What do the media have to say about the fact that the UK has recently sold arms to all five countries of origin topping the UK list of asylum applicants in 2001? This, despite the fact that, in each case, violent military conflict remains the dominant root cause of refugee flight. More generally, what emphasis is placed on adverse conditions in countries of origin — poverty, human rights abuses, global income disparity, conflict and torture — in articles concerned with asylum and immigration?

Randall also notes that, "The issue of asylum and immigration is reported in terms of a 'threat' and 'invasion' *despite a lack of statistical evidence supporting such dramatic claims.*" (Emphasis added). For example, the huge number of crimes committed against immigrants — from torture, forced eviction and illegal detention in their countries of origin, to property abuse and physical violence in the UK

— is given far less attention than the much smaller proportion of crimes committed by immigrants themselves.

In terms of global context and wider coverage, the study noted:

- "Comparative analyses of immigration and asylum worldwide are barely referenced at all."
  - When this does briefly emerge, the issue in all cases involves a positive commentary on the strict exclusion policies of other European countries, and not, as might be expected, any analysis of the UK's comparatively low intake.
  - Discussion of the number of refugees and migrants entering and living in non-western countries is completely absent from all ninety articles studied.
- "Important root causes of immigration and refugee flight, such as war, torture, poverty and oppression, are referred to fleetingly, if at all."

- "The effects of poverty and inequality in sending countries are deemed unworthy of mention in any newspaper despite extensive coverage detailing politicians' condemnations of 'bogus' and 'illegal' 'economic immigration'."
- "War and violent conflict are mentioned in just eight of ninety articles in all three newspapers, a very low figure when compared with the thirty-seven articles discussing the relatively minor issue of asylum seeker accommodation."
- 6% of the articles studied from these papers covered the situation in sending countries, reflecting a "general failure" to discuss such aspects.
- "The fundamental macro issue of demography — indicating both the insignificant effects of immigration on population growth and its potentially positive effects on the UK's aging population — is not mentioned throughout the case study."
- "Macro issues that might embarrass

powerful state-corporate interests are also ignored or neglected. Two major examples include the impacts of the arms trade and economic trade liberalisation. The former receives no mention at all, while the latter is hinted at (indirectly) in one piece in the Guardian."

o The majority of articles that discussed human rights as a theme covered the same issue, about UK consiering withdrawing from the European Convention on Human Rights in order to justify the exclusion of certain asylum seekers. Yet, while a human rights issue, "it is placed in the context of exclusion policies and 'bogus' asylum applicants. This limits to just three articles any mention of human rights abuses in the country of origin — abuses that might have caused the original application to be made, and which cast a far less negative light on the subject of asylum and immigration."

In looking at the media coverage, an interesting observation was made:

An interesting, perhaps ironic, footnote to the thematic results involves the eight references made to media coverage. Both the Guardian and the Independent provide a number of articles denouncing what they describe as the essentially racist coverage of tabloid and right-wing newspapers, including the third news outlet in this case study, the Daily Telegraph. The latter does not follow this theme and has no articles mentioning media coverage.

However, as this case study shows, although opinions expressed on immigration themes certainly illustrate ideological differences between "right-wing" newspapers such as the Telegraph and the more "liberal" Independent/Guardian, there is clear conformity when it comes to deciding +which+ themes to discuss — a fundamental conformity.... Comment on this aspect of coverage does not feature in the Guardian/Independent articles criticising media performance.

While a full third of the case studies afforded view points from non-governmental organizations (NGOs) (politicians being afforded the most coverage) giving the sense of balance, Randall notes that, "a closer analysis shows that politicians remain overwhelmingly the agenda-setters in these articles with NGO representatives very seldom initiating the subject of the news item. Their role is very much confined to reaction and comment."

This general trend reveals how view points representing those who have influence are the ones that typically make it into mainstream discourse. "Analysis of media sourcing demonstrates that UK newsgathering has a strong symbiotic relationship with political elites ensuring that a substantial number of articles are formed around government press releases and statements of policy. Groups without recourse to large public relations resources — such as asylum seekers, refugees and the predominantly small NGOs that represent them — tend not to set the agenda for issues under discussion."

We therefore get a strange situation whereby ideologically distinct newspapers "focus on aspects of immigration and asylum that concur with the priorities of the political elite.... [representing] an extremely narrow range of information and opinion". The "significant avoidance and omission of important themes and issues that should form regular and central points of reference" leads to a support of an agenda of the political elite, even if that is not the intention.

Opinions Reflect Hype — Especially During Election Time

Almost a year and a half since the above was written, the hype has remained. And as the

British 2005 elections have drawn closer, the issue of immigration and asylum has been one of the issues discussed (out of an extremely small number of issues, it has to be added).

In a poll on immigration conducted for ITV News in the UK (April 2005), some interesting observations were made:
- 73% of people thought too many immigrants were allowed into the UK – and just 3% believed that not enough were allowed;
- 75% believe immigrants put a strain on public services;
- 39% of people believed immigrants bring disease to the UK;
- 25% felt migrants make Britain a thriving multicultural society;

In testing some of these views, ITV noted the following:

- In the 2002/3 tax year, 272,000 people came to the UK from across the world and were given a national insurance number. Just

8% went on to claim benefits;

○ Between May and December 2004, 133,000 from the new EU countries registered to work in the UK. Just 21 of them were allowed to claim benefits (0.016%!)

○ On HIV, the Health Protection Agency does estimate that 75% of new heterosexual infections in 2003 were probably acquired in Africa. On Tuberculosis (TB), public health figures said 67% of TB infections were born abroad in 2002. But targeted screening at Heathrow airport found just 100 cases in 175,000 tests in 2004 (0.057%!). The British Medical Association said it has seen no evidence of a health tourism phenomenon.

For a long time, but increasingly during election times, spear-headed by right-wing parties such as the Conservatives and tabloid media, scares of immigration being "out of control" are returning.

For sure, there have been isolated incidents that cause much concern, such as the recent case of a <u>failed asylum seeker killing a police officer and conspiring to create the deadly poison ricin</u> (though it seems police foiled that in time).

However, using terrorism to add to the asylum and immigration hysteria just creates more fear and animosity. In effect, it also suggests that almost all (especially brown-skinned) asylum seekers and immigrants are potential terrorists.

(It has even got to the point where I know some fellow Asians in UK who also say that immigration is out of control, though they talk not of people from their own ethnicities and backgrounds of course, but of "others".)

Furthermore, the impact on public services, like health, of obesity, excessive sugar/beef-based diets, tobacco and other unhealthy items far outweighs the impacts immigrants have on such services. (For more details on these impacts, see this site's section on <u>behind consumption and consumerism</u>, and on <u>causes of hunger</u>.) These other problems not only affect British people, but also have a significant impact on other parts of the world. Notably, there has almost been *nothing* discussed on these other issues during the same election campaign, in either a national or international context. Instead, immigration has been publicized as a more important issue.

United Europe

The European Union has had policies to control immigration from non-member countries. Spain for example seems to be facing a larger number of immigrants from Morocco and other North African countries where people want to escape their politically conflict-torn countries and seek a better standard of living in Europe. However, <u>many people are dying</u> trying to achieve this.

The preceding paragraph was written some 8 years ago, in 1998. In September 2006, similar issues still exist. *Inter Press Service* reports on <u>many issues continuing today</u>. For example, Spain recently "threatened to deport illegal immigrants residing within its borders." In addition, "The British government says it is considering restricting access to nationals of Bulgaria and Romania—if and when the two countries gain admission to the EU."

As the European Union has grown, it is common

to hear concerns in UK for example, at the rising number of people from East Europe. The fear is the threat to job security and downward pressure on wages, which are understandable concerns. The underlying context of what makes this possible—the corporate drive for a more open, free market system within the EU, that will see winners and losers, and that also tends towards the lowest common denominators—is hardly discussed.

Interestingly, *IPS* also adds that "Since 2004, when most Eastern Europe countries joined the EU, over 427,000 East Europeans, about two-thirds from Poland, have registered for employment in Britain. At the same time, Western Europe is now more inclined to hire Eastern Europeans both for skilled and unskilled jobs than Asians and Africans."

Some human rights activists say that the European restrictions need to be modified or African nations need to overcome their under-development in order to alleviate some of these problems. However, <u>the current form of</u>

globalization doesn't look like it will immediately help the developing nations.

Economics, Poverty And Immigrant Scapegoats

It is generally believed that those immigrants who have had the courage to leave one country and move to another are often enterprising and entrepreneurial, even if poor. As such, in many countries, immigrants often set up small businesses. They however, become easy targets when the general economic conditions in that host country worsen.

In other cases, people become immigrants because they have fled worsening conditions or persecution. In that situation, although they may live in another country, it may initially be quite difficult to adapt and change practices and customs. In such situations immigrants are clearly seen as different and in worsening economic times can be seen as sapping away resources that could otherwise have been used for local populations.

In the 1970s and 80s, Indian and Pakistani immigrants in the UK for example faced constant racist harassment and jokes about their small businesses. Many Indian and Pakistani communities escaping turmoil in East Africa were technically allowed to come to the UK but very quickly local populations became concerned and held numerous protests. While these communities have managed to weather this and many are now quite successful, the new wave of immigrants, Polish in particular it seems, face a new wave of hostility.

During the global financial crisis at the end of the 1990s, East Asia was particularly affected. This resulted in a wave of anti immigrant sentiments, for example in Indonesia there was a wave of violence against Chinese immigrants.

In May 2008, <u>South Africa saw a wave of anti immigrant violence</u>, as extremely poor South Africans turned against thousands of immigrants from other parts of Africa, killing some 50, and forcing thousands to leave.

In these and many other situations not mentioned here, anti-immigrant sentiment typically comes to the fore when economic conditions deteriorate. They are an easy target and either lies or exaggerations can contribute to fear, anxiety and ultimately hatred.

As discussed earlier mainstream media coverage in some countries, even places like Britain, makes it easy to stir up hysterical stories about immigration which helps direct the conversation and policies towards who can be "toughest" on immigration.

When economic conditions get harder, these views are easier to digest and adopt and deeper causes, of why people immmigrate in the first place, are less discussed. As a result, empathy and understanding for the situation and conditions immigrants face is easily lost.

There are indeed cases where some immigrant

groups may come to countries like Britain under the mistaken and exaggerated understanding that if you cannot find work the government will pay for you to live (I remember on various vacations in developing countries being asked if this is true!). This may be tempting for some groups that face much hardship, but it will be understandable in that case that local populations will not look too kindly on this attempt to get a "free ride." Where this happens, it is unfortunately too easy for populist anti-immigrant sentiment to exaggerate that "all" immigrants want this.

Other times, policy does indeed seem to favor struggling immigrants over struggling local populations; it could be argued that local populations have had more opportunity than immigrant populations, and so the latter may benefit from some temporary assistance, but local populations are not going to accept that easily leaving policy makers feel they have little choice but to appear tough on immigration.

Chapter 3
Racism

Racism is the belief that characteristics and abilities can be attributed to people simply on the basis of their race and that some racial groups are superior to others. Racism and discrimination have been used as powerful weapons encouraging fear or hatred of others in times of conflict and war, and even during economic downturns. **What is racism? Visible and invisible characteristics**

What does being a racist mean? What is racism?3 We prefer the ideas that the teenagers we interviewed gave us over any manual on the subject. According to them, racism is:

- discriminating against a person because of their color or race
- not interacting with black people
- fighting with someone because he or she is from another country

- only valuing people from your own group
- associating prejudices with a group that we call a race
- classifying human beings
- classifying human beings using prejudices
- classifying human beings on a hierarchical scale from best to worst
- attributing a series of "good" and "bad" characteristics to a person according to their physical aspect
- hate identified with a series of prejudices
- inferiorizing
- insinuating that we are not the same people as they are

Thinking about racism

The ideas quoted are very relevant and interesting for understanding what racism is, but the teenagers themselves expanded on these ideas and complicated what they associated with the concept of racism when we asked them to recount situations in their lives that they had perceived as racist or discriminatory. They told us about some direct experiences and about other indirect ones:

3 To answer these questions, we offer two activities: Definitions of racism I and Definitions of racism II.

a) direct experiences:
- contempt
- insults
- expressions such as "go back to your country"
- physical aggression
- ridicule
- denying favors
- rudeness
- intimidation
- harrassment
- physical threats

b) indirect experiences:
- being assigned to a specific group and because of that
feeling that people assume that you will behave the same
way they have seen other people in this same

group behave
- feeling that teachers undervalue your capabilities or future possibilities, seeing yourself directed more frequently toward training-type academic orientations than toward the university
- racist statements, such as "Latinos only come here to steal," made in class by the teachers
- advice to students with immigrant origins to avoid interacting with people from their country of origin, in order to help them to integrate more quickly, as well as the opposite advice, to interact with people from your country of origin
- the perception that, in schools where immigrants are a minority, they undergo greater discrimination than in schools where there is a larger group
- the perception that racist behavior tends to

take place when the aggressors act as a group
- the perception that adults with immigrant origins (from their same places of origin) do not have access to all different kinds of jobs and find themselves limited to sectors such as construction
- establishing a direct relation between immigration in Spain and the process of Spanish colonization in America, seeing the causes of present-day immigration in the effects of the process of colonization by Spain that their countries underwent in the past
- the perception that these adults with immigrant origins (from their same places of origin) work more hours for lower salaries

Analyzing the critical incident

How is racism reflected in the critical incident? Directly, indirectly or both? How do you think young people would react to these kinds of racism? What consequences do they have? Is there any difference between a direct act of racism and an indirect one?

This variety of perceptions broadens and refines enormously what the teenagers themselves associated directly with the concepts of racism and discrimination. Now we will attempt to offer a framework of reference that will help us to understand the complexity of these ideas and to relate them to one another.

In order it has also fostered inequality and discrimination for centuries, as well as influencing how we relate to other human beings:

We understand **racism** to mean:
a) **Social behavior and the socio-political ideas and institutions that**

support it, including a series of different and complex mechanisms learned
from childhood onward.

b) **This behavior consists of classifying people in groups,** that is, of using
what we believe about a group to refer to individuals, **based on real or
imaginary differences;** what is important is that these differences are
believable and believed.

c) **These differences are associated with behaviors (also real or
imaginary)** of the people in the group **and they are generalized** to all the
members of the group.

d) **The objective of the classification is to justify a hierarchy among the
groups,** making it seem that some are better than others.

e) **This hierarchy is what makes us accept the privileges of the people in
one group over people in another group,** in terms of social goods: power,
prestige, and money.

f) This hierarchy also has the power to make the blame for disadvantages fall on the victim, because it makes everyone believe the explanation that some people are worth more than others and therefore deserve more and better, simply because they are classified in one group and not in another.

It is important to point out that the kinds of differences used for classifying people into groups vary widely. Physical differences are some of the most frequently used reasons, *because they have the power and efficacy of marking people by sight.*
However, in Europe basically, a wide variety of differences, such as religion, mother tongue, place of origin, sex, c

Racism In Europe

"Europe has a regional human rights architecture which is unrivaled elsewhere in the world", Amnesty International notes in their

2010 report on the Europe and Central Asia region. But the human rights watchdog also adds that as well as guarding a proud reputation as a beacon of human rights, "it is sadly still the case, however, that the reality of protection from human rights abuses for many of those within its borders falls short of the rhetoric." In recent years, one of those forms of abuses has been in the area of race, often growing with changing economic circumstances and increased immigration to the region.

From the institutionalized racism especially in colonial times, when racial beliefs — even eugenics — were not considered something wrong, to recent times where the effects of neo-Nazism is still felt, Europe is a complex area with many cultures in a relatively small area of land that has seen many conflicts throughout history. (Many of these conflicts have had trade, resources and commercial rivalry at their core, but national identities have often added fuel to some of these conflicts.)

Racism has also been used to justify exploitation, even using "pseudo-science":

Debates over the origins of racism often suffer from a lack of clarity over the term. Many conflate recent forms of racism with earlier forms of ethnic and national conflict. In most cases ethno-national conflict seems to owe to conflict over land and strategic resources. In some cases ethnicity and nationalism were harnessed to wars between great religious empires (for example, the Muslim Turks and the Catholic Austro-Hungarians). As Benedict Anderson has suggested in *Imagined Communities*, ethnic identity and ethno-nationalism became a source of conflict within such empires with the rise of print-capitalism.

In its modern form, racism evolved in tandem with European exploration and conquest of much of the rest of the world, and especially after Christopher Columbus reached the Americas. As new peoples were encountered, fought, and ultimately subdued, theories about "race" began to develop, and these helped many to justify the differences in position and treatment of people whom they categorized as belonging to different races (see Eric Wolf's *Europe and the People Without History*).

Another possible source of racism is the misunderstanding of Charles Darwin's theories of evolution. Some took Darwin's theories to imply that since some "races" were more civilized, there must be a biological basis for the difference. At the same time they appealed to biological theories of moral and intellectual traits to justify racial oppression. There is a great deal of controversy about race and intelligence, in part because the concepts of both race and IQ are themselves controversial.

— Racism, Wikipedia, The Free Encyclopedia, May 1, 2004

In "the century of total war", and the new millenium, Europe is seeing an alarming resurgence in xenophobia and racial hatred.

A short review from the *Inter Press Service* highlights the rise of neo-Nazism in 2000 in Europe and suggests that "far from being a fringe activity, racism, violence and neo-nationalism have become normal in some communities. The problems need to tackled much earlier, in schools and with social programmes."

Ethnic minorities and different cultures in one country can often be used as a scapegoat for the majority during times of economic crisis.

That is one reason why Nazism became so popular.

In France, May 2002, the success of far right politician Le Pen in the run for leadership (though he lost out in the end) sent a huge shockwave throughout Europe, about how easy it was for far right parties to come close to getting power if there is complacency in the democratic processes and if participation is reduced.

In various places throughout Western Europe, in 2002, as Amnesty International highlights, there has been a rise in racist attacks and sentiments against both Arabs and Jews, in light of the increasing hostilities in the Middle East.

Earlier in 1998, in an area of Germany a right wing racist party won an unprecedented number of votes.

In Austria, the Freedom Party was able to secure the majority of the cabinet posts. The party is an extreme far right party, whose leader, Jorg Heider, has been accused of sympathetic statements towards the Nazis. The European Union has reacted to this indicating that Austria's participation may be in jeopardy. This Guardian Special Report has much more in-depth coverage.

In Italy, there are attempts to try and deal with the rise in undocumented immigrants from Tunisia. The reactions from the right wing have been labeled by some as being "openly racist".

Into 2010 and problems of racism in Italy continue. For example, a wave of violence against African farm workers in southern Italy left some 70 people injured. This resulted in police having to evacuate over 300 workers from the region. The workers were easy targets being exploited as fruit pickers living in difficult conditions. They earn "starvation wages" according to a BBC reporter, doing "backbreaking work which Italians do not want" in a labor market controlled by the local mafia.

Spain has seen increased racial violence. The growing economy invites immigrants from North African countries such as Morocco. However, the poor conditions that immigrants have had to endure and the already racially charged region has led to friction and confrontations.

In 1997, *Human Rights Watch* noted that, "The U.K. has one of the highest levels of racially-motivated violence and harassment in Western Europe, and the problem is getting worse." In April 1999, London saw two bombs explode in predominantly ethnic minority areas, in the space of one week, where a Nazi group has claimed responsibility. The summer of 2001 saw many race-related riots in various parts of northern England.

For over a decade, immigration issues have been headlines in the UK. The nature of the discussions bear a clear racial dimension as well as hostility to Eastern Europeans, such as those from Poland. Anti-immigrant rhetoric has also contributed to increasing interest in racist political parties such as the British National Party. This also, predictably, has increased as the global financial crisis impacts more of Britain's population.

Anti immigration sentiment has also been seen in Switzerland as the country has repeatedly tightened its asylum policy due to concerns about increasing numbers of illegal migrants.

Greece has one of the worst records in the European Union for racism against ethnic minorities, according to the BBC. Anti-immigrant sentiment has long been high, especially against ethnic Albanians, who form the largest minority. Until the 1990s, the BBC notes, Greece had been an extremely homogenous society. With the fall of communism many immigrants from Eastern Europe came to Greece. Albanians especially have been targetted by a lot of racist sentiment. Some hostage taking by a few Albanians in recent years has not helped the situation.

Russia has seen violent anti-racism on the rise in recent years together with the rise of neo-Nazism (which is a cruel irony given the immense death toll the Soviet Union suffered at the hands of Nazi Germany during World War II). Although the previous report is from 2006, Amnesty International's 2010 report shows that despite greater recognition of the problem, effective programs to tackle the issue still do not exist.

So far, the above represents an incredibly tiny number of examples and details. Many, many more events haven't been mentioned, as it is admittedly difficult to keep up with all the different items. For more details and up-to-date information, one web site to check out the UK-based *Institute of Race Relations* and their subsection attempting to document the rising support for the extreme-Right in local and central government in Europe, building on a platform of populist anti-immigrant policies.

Back to top

Racism In Australia

In 1987, a sensational "discovery" was made by a Sydney University team, led by Australia's most celebrated pre-historian, Professor D J Mulvaney. They reported that the Australian population in 1788 was 750,000, or three times the previous estimate. They concluded that more than 600,000 people had died as result of white settlement.

— *John Pilger,* Cathy Freeman's broad Olympic smile is being used to conceal a multitude of Australia's original sins, July 10, 2000

In June 1998, One Nation, an Australian nationalist party in Queensland won 25

<u>percent</u> of the votes with their main lines at fighting immigration by non-whites. This was made possible where unemployment was been high and where it was easy to convince the people that immigrants were taking their jobs, as it would serve to be a convenient excuse and avenue to vent frustration. In a speech the party leader said that Australia was "in danger of being swamped" by Asians and she also questioned the special welfare benefits for Australia's Aborigines. The reaction to that meant **the same party won only 6 percent of the votes** two months later, in the State elections.

Australia has also had a very racist past in which apartheid has been practiced and where indigenous Aboriginal people have lost almost all their land and suffered many prejudices. In the past, the notorious policy that led to the <u>Stolen Generation</u> was practiced. This was the institutionalized attempt to prevent Aboriginal children (and thus future generations) from being socialized into Aboriginal culture. (This also occurred in various parts of the Americas too.)

Aborigines are the poorest group in Australia and suffer from very much preventable diseases. For more about these issues, you can start at these harrowing reports from <u>John Pilger</u> a prominent Australian journalist who has been critical of many western policies.

The Sydney 2000 Olympics also brought some of Australia's racist past and present <u>to the fore</u>. (On the positive side, many parts of Australia's rich diversity in people is slowly helping relieve prejudism. However, some more traditional and conservative politicians are still openly racist.)

In 2008, a study found that Australians in general are welcoming of diversity but some 1 in 10 Australians still hold racist views — a ratio likely to be less than in some European countries, but still high the lead researcher noted. Muslims were most feared or loathed for "not belonging", and followed by indigenous Australians and Africans.

In 2009 and 2010, there were increasing racist attacks against Indians with many Indians in Melbourne fearing racist attacks and lynchings were increasing. It even led to the Indian government issuing an advisory warning about the dangers of traveling to Melbourne.

Back to top

Racism In Africa

A number of nations in Africa are at war or civil war, or have been very recently, just few years after they have gained their independence from former colonial countries.

While most of the conflicts have resources at their core and involve a number of non-African nations and corporations, additional fuel is added to the conflict by stirring up ethnic differences and enticing hatred. (Also not that the artificial boundaries imposed in Africa by European colonialism and imperialism during the divide and rule policies has further exacerbated this situation and plays an enormous role in the root causes of these conflicts compared to what mainstream media presents.)

In Zimbabwe, there has been increasing racism against the white farmers, due to poverty and lack of land ownership by Africans.

South Africa until recently suffered from Apartheid, which legally segregated the African population from the Europeans.

For more about conflicts in Africa, check out this site's section on Africa.

Back to top

Racism In The Middle East

In a number of countries in the Middle East, discriminatory practice has been commonplace, mostly against foreign workers who work in low wage conditions, such as domestic workers. Reports of taking away foreign worker's passports and treating them as second class citizens are unfortunately commonplace.

Inter Press Service (IPS) describes how Lebanon has these discrimination problems even though it is often considered relatively open compared to its neighbors, due to freedoms enjoyed by women. For example, people of color face discrimination at work and away from work, often not allowed at some beaches or clubs, or allowed with various restrictions. In addition, property rights are severely curtailed, even for Palestinians who are the same race, but not nationals.

Worsening discrimination in recent months seen at various beaches in Lebanon was "symptomatic of the widespread racism that exists in Lebanon" says Ali Fakhri, communication director at Indyact, a Lebanese NGO finding that all of the 20 beaches investigated barred domestic workers from Asia and Africa from using their facilities. Fakhri also feels that the culture of discrimination is socially accepted in Lebanon, and is seen in the government and private sector as well as among individuals, according to IPS and the discrimination/racism does not only target people of color, but is also class oriented and sectarian.

Highlighting the effects a legal system can have on culture, a lawyer also interviewed by IPS notes that "The Lebanese constitution states that all Lebanese are equal in the eyes of the law, but no mention is made of the rights of foreigners." In the absence of a unified civil law, such discrimination will continue she adds: "The Lebanese legal system follows different rules of law that vary from one community to the other. It is a situation that naturally leads to inequality among people."

As well as these cultural practices, there has also been a geopolitical dimension:

For a long time there has been resentment by many in the Middle East at the policies of America in their region. For many of the more extremist factions, this has turned into a form of racism as well, where many things that are Western are hated or despised.

The situation of Palestine and Israel is also very contentious. While Arabs and Jews technically do not belong to different races, their religious and cultural differences and the political history of the region has contributed to extremities and tensions — by perhaps a minority, but perhaps an influential and often vocal and violent minority — resulting in prejudice on both sides.

With the terrible acts of terrorism committed by terrorists in America, on September 11, 2001, there has additionally been an outpouring of violent racial hatred by a minority of people in Western countries against people that look Middle Eastern (some who are not Middle Eastern, such as Indians, have even been beaten or killed). Furthermore, with the American-led attacks in Afghanistan in retaliation for those terrorist attacks, from Egypt to Pakistan, there have been minorities of people who have protested violently in the streets, and also committed racist acts, attacking anything that appears Western, from Western citizens, to even UNICEF and other UN buildings.

Yet, this is more complex than just a clash of religions and race, as deeper an issue is the geopolitical and economic activities of the past decades and centuries that have fueled these social tensions. See this web site's section on the Middle East for more on that.

Back to top

Racism In Asia

In Cambodia, there has been a strong anti-Vietnamese sentiment.

In Indonesia there has been a lot of violence against the affluent Chinese population who have been blamed for economic problems that have plagued the country in recent years.

As noted by Wikipedia in an article on racism, "until 2003, Malaysia enforced discriminatory laws limiting access to university education for Chinese students who are citizens by birth of Malaysia, and many other laws explicitly favoring bumiputras (Malays) remain in force."

In India, there has long been discrimination against what is considered the lowest class in Hinduism, the Dalits, or untouchables, as well as sectarian and religious violence. Although it has been outlawed by the Indian Constitution, the caste system was a way to structure inequality into the system itself. And while outlawed, the social barriers it creates is still prevalent in rural areas where most Indians live. It also features in the view of Hindu extremists and traditionalists.

At various times, there have also been tensions between different religious groups, such as Hindus and Muslims with both sides having their fair share of extremists. While this is not racism, technically — as people of all classes are of the same race — the prejudice that had come with the caste system is quite similar to what is seen with racism.

Back to top

Racism In North America

A report from *Survival International* about the plight of the Innu people in Canada also reveals how racism can be a factor. In the words of the authors, the "report reveals how racist government policies, under the guise of benevolent 'progress', have crippled the Innu of eastern Canada — a once self-sufficient and independent people." (While this report is about the problems of an indigenous people in Canada, it is a common story throughout history for many peoples and cultures.)

In the US, racism is a well known issue. From racial profiling to other issues such as affirmative action, police brutality against minorities and the history of slavery and the rising resentment against immigrants.

The American Anthropological Association

produced a short video providing an overview of how prevailing ideas in science, government and culture intersected throughout history to shape American concept of race today:

The Story of Race, Understanding Race, American Anthropological Association, July 13, 2009

Since the horrific terrorist attacks on the United States on September 11, 2001, Security concerns have understandably increased, but so too has racial profiling, discrimination etc. In the early aftermath of the attacks some Americans that were understandably outraged and horrified, even attacked some members of the Sikh community where at least one was even killed, because they resembled certain types of Muslims, with beards and turbans. Various people of Middle East or South Asian origin have faced controversial detentions or questionings by officials at American airports. This web site's section on the war against terror has more details on these aspects.

It was a historic moment for America when they voted in their first black president, Barack

Obama, given America's history. Yet, it seems that some of his policies have met with near hysterical opposition (his attempt to push a somewhat more inclusive health system has been decried as socialist, or even communist, for example).

One can't help but see the increasing criticism from right wing segments having a racist, almost coordinated, undertone to it. He is Christian, although his middle name is Hussein, which right wingers have used to claim he is Muslim, anti-Christ and so on, which further fuels racial and discriminatory sentiments.

Leonard Zeskind, head of the Institute for Research and Education on Human Rights, pointed out that the anti-Obama "opposition" contains many different political elements:

[Elements of anti-Obama opposition] include ultra-conservative Republicans of both the Pat Buchanan and free market variety; anti-tax Tea Party libertarians from the Ron Paul camp;

Christian right activists intent on re-molding the country into their kind of Kingdom; birth certificate conspiracy theorists, anti-immigrant nativists of the armed Minuteman and the policy wonk variety; third party "constitutionalists"; and white nationalists of both the citizens councils and the Stormfront national socialist variety.

— *Bill Berkowitz*, US: White Supremacists Crash Anti-Obama Tea Party, Inter Press Service, December 22, 2009

Back to top

The Lure Of Adolph Hitler And Neo-Nazism

It seems that many people who join supremacist groups do so at a young age, and a lot of recruiting by these various hate groups are targeted at children. A reformed skinhead adds how easy it can be for some people, to be recruited into these groups, especially children.

On the anniversary of Adolph Hitler's birthday in April 1999, a planned killing spree at the now infamous Columbine High School in America by two children claimed the lives of many fellow school mates. It is reported that they were targeting ethnic minorities and were involved in some Nazi related activities.

Side Note»

In USA, the Oklahoma City bombing in 1995 (incidentally, the day before the birthday of Adolph Hitler) triggered anti-Muslim sentiments, even though it was not an Islamic group at all. The previous link reports that there was a 60% increase in discrimination of Muslims in the USA.

And during the week of Adolf Hitler's birthday, in 1999, neo-Nazi groups were suspected of planting two nail bombs that exploded in predominantly ethnic minority areas of London. The following week, a gay bar in London's Soho area was also bombed killing at least 3 people. The fact that the Stephen Lawrence case, which, in UK is one of the perhaps most infamous on-going cases of racism in the police force and has received much attention at the time of this bombing could be more than coincidence.

Back to top

Racism Against Gypsies

One group of people that often go unnoticed when it comes to racism and discrimination are Gypsies. In Europe they have been persecuted to a similar extent as the Jews throughout history, including World War II and even now they are largely mistreated or ignored.

Back to top

Immigration

> *Please note that this section has moved into its own page, immigration.*

Back to top

The Internet And Racism

And while the World Wide Web is a great proponent for the ideals of free speech, it can also be a breeding ground harboring hatred. This is very serious as the number of hate sites that have sprung up in the recent years is shocking and also increasing at an alarming rate.

There has been much talk of Internet sites hosting hate material. Some groups such asHateWatch have gone as far as buying racist domain names so that real racists cannot buy these domains themselves!

For more about the Internet and free speech, check out this site's section on human rights and the Internet. It has some useful links to additional sites and material.

Back to top

Globalization And Racism

As globalization in its current form expands, so too does the inequality that accompanies it, as discussed throughout the Trade, Economy, & Related Issues section on this web site. Rising inequality can result in an increase in racial bias for scapegoating or advancing xenophobic and isolationist tendencies.

During French and British Imperial days for example, racial bias was ingrained within the culture itself (as explored in great detail by Edward Said, in his books such as *Orientalism*(Vintage Books, 1979) and *Culture & Imperialism* (Vintage Books, 1993)). However, an element of this is also seen in today's period of globalization, with what A. Sivanandan describes as the increasing "xenophobic culture of globalisation" seen in some parts of the world:

Racism has always been both an instrument of discrimination and a tool of exploitation. But it manifests itself as a cultural phenomenon, susceptible to cultural solutions, such as multicultural education and the promotion of ethnic identities.

Tackling the problem of cultural inequality, however, does not by itself redress the problem of economic inequality. Racism is conditioned by economic imperatives, but negotiated through culture: religion, literature, art, science and the media.

... Once, they demonised the blacks to justify slavery. Then they demonised the "coloureds" to justify colonialism. Today, they demonise asylum seekers to justify the ways of globalism. And, in the age of the media, of spin, demonisation sets out the parameters of popular culture within which such exclusion finds its own rationale — usually under the guise of xenophobia, the fear of strangers.

— A. Sivanandan, Poverty is the new black, The Guardian, August 17, 2001

With expanding globalization, the demands for more skilled workers, especially in North America, Europe and elsewhere (while they cut back on education spending themselves, little by little), has led to increased efforts to attract foreign workers — but filtered, based on skill. At the same time, this increases resentment by those in those nations who are not benefitting from globalization.

Additionally, those trying to escape authoritarian regimes etc are finding it harder and harder to get into these countries, due to tighter immigration policies. Hence it is harder to immigrate to the wealthier nations unless,

says Liz Fekete, "these citizens are part of the chosen few: highly-skilled computer wizards, doctors and nurses trained at Third World expense and sought after by the West. Global migration management strategy saps the Third World and the former Soviet bloc of its economic lifeblood, by creaming off their most skilled and educated workforces." From the perspective of globalization, Liz continues, "the skills pool, not the genes pool, is key."

Immigrants face numerous criticisms and challenges; It is difficult enough often, to get into another nation as mentioned above. If one succeeds, then additional struggles (some to naturally be expected, of course) are faced:

- Living in a new country can be daunting, especially when the cultural differences are great.
- As a result it can be expected that an immigrant would try to maintain some semblance of their own culture in their new

country of stay.
- Or, due to fears of racism or due to the culture shock it would be expected that immigrant communities would form as a way to deal with this and as a means to help each other through.
- By doing this, sometimes they face criticism of not integrating and of "sticking with their own kind";
- Yet, on the other hand, if they do integrate in some way, they face critique from certain types of environmentalists and others of contributing to environmental degradation by increasing their consumption to the high levels typical of the host nation.
  - (And if environmental degradation is the concern, then it would make sense that one of the main issues at hand to address would be the consumption itself and its roots, regardless of who is doing it — in this context
  - That is, if the host nation had different modes of consumptions, immigrants would likely follow those too.

- Hence, singling out immigrants for being a factor in environmental degradation is often unfair, and itself hints of prejudice and of attitudes — intentional or not — almost like "stay out; we want to maintain and not share our lifestyle and standards of living; we recognize it is wasteful but if not too many are doing it, then it is ok" etc.)
- For more about these issues of resource consumption, blaming the poor and immigrants etc, see this web site's section debating population and consumption issues.

Back to top

UN's World Conference On Racism, 2001

A UN Global Conference to discuss racism, racial discrimination, xenophobia and related intolerance was held from 31st August to 7 September 2001.

While it was brave enough for the United

Nations to attempt to hold such a meeting, it proved to be a heated challenge. While all nations are good at being critical of others (and often very accurately, although often not!), when it comes to one's own criticisms, most would be uncomfortable to say the least. As an example:

- United States and Europe were against effective discussions of slavery reparations (and sent in only low-level delegates — a possible sign on how they really feel about this conference, and what it is about)
- Israel and United States were against discussing the possibility that Zionism is racist against Palestinians, causing both to walk out of the conference altogether
- India was against including discussions about caste-based discrimination
- Some Arab nations were against discussions on oppression of Kurds or Arab slave trade
- etc.

A watered down declaration was eventually

made.

Such an eventful week shows how far we all have to go! It is also a detailed issue, and the following links may provide more details:

- **World Conference Against Racism** is the official United Nations web site
- **OneWorld.net Special Report on Racism** provides a huge number of articles from all sorts of NGO and other partners.

Chapter 4
Terrorism

Terrorism is the systematic use of violence (terror) as a means of coercion for political purposes. In the international community, terrorism has no legally binding, criminal law definition.[1][2] Common definitions of terrorism refer only to those violent acts which are intended to create fear (terror); are perpetrated for a religious, political, or ideological goal; and deliberately target or disregard the safety of non-combatants (civilians). Some definitions now include acts of unlawful violence and war. The use of similar tactics by criminal organizations for protection rackets or to enforce a code of silence is usually not labeled terrorism, though these same actions may be labeled terrorism when done by a politically motivated group.

The word "terrorism" is politically and emotionally charged,[3] and this greatly compounds the difficulty of providing a precise definition. Studies have found over 100 definitions of "terrorism".[4][5] The concept of terrorism may be controversial as it is often used by state authorities (and individuals with access to state support) to delegitimize political or other opponents,[6] and potentially legitimize the state's own use of armed force against opponents (such use of force may be described as "terror" by opponents of the state).[6][7] At the same time, the reverse is also used where states perpetrate state terrorism.

Terrorism has been practiced by a broad array of political organizations to further their objectives. It has been practiced by both right-wing and left-wing political parties, nationalistic groups, religious groups, revolutionaries, and ruling governments.[8] An abiding characteristic is the indiscriminate use of violence against noncombatants for the purpose of gaining publicity for a group, cause, or individual. The symbolism of terrorism can exploit human fear to help achieve these goals.[9]

Origin of term

"Terrorism" comes from the French word *terrorisme*,[10] and originally referred specifically to state terrorism as practiced by the French government during the Reign of terror. The French word *terrorisme* in turn derives from the Latin verb *terreō* meaning "I frighten".[11] The *terror cimbricus* was a panic and state of emergency in Rome in response to the approach of warriors of the Cimbri tribe in 105 BC. The Jacobins cited this precedent when imposing a Reign of Terror during the French Revolution.[12][13] After the Jacobins lost power, the word "terrorist" became a term of abuse.[6] Although "terrorism" originally referred to acts committed by a government, currently it usually refers to the killing of innocent people[14] for political purposes in such a way as to create a media spectacle. This meaning can be traced back to Sergey Nechayev, who described himself as a "terrorist".[15] Nechayev founded the Russian terrorist group "People's Retribution" (Народная расправа) in 1869.[16]

In November 2004, a <u>United Nations Secretary General</u> report described terrorism as any act "intended to cause death or serious bodily harm to civilians or non-combatants with the purpose of intimidating a population or compelling a government or an international organization to do or abstain from doing any act".[17]

History of terrorism

In the previous video we looked at the facts and the map of terrorism and it's victims. In this video we're going to look at the history of terrorism. Non state actors using terrorism. It's not really new. Even in pre-modern days, there were groups and individuals that used political violence against the authorities and elite. Think of a group we now call The Assassins. Who in the late 11th century in the Middle East killed governors, political and military leaders in order to create alliances or as an act of retribution. So nothing new and yes they were to assassinate something or somebody, stems from a group which we now would label a terrorist one. But most descriptions of modern day terrorism starts with the anarchists that are associated with the propaganda of the deed from the French propaganda par le fait. A group or network or movement that was active since the 1870s, 1880s. Another slogan associated with the early, modern day terrorism, is the slogan [FOREIGN], from the internal Macedonian Revolutionary Organization that was fighting the Ottoman rule in the late nineteenth, early twentieth centuries. So even more than a century ago there were many different groups using different tactics, slogans and with different political backgrounds, ranging from the extreme left to nationalist separatists. And some killed heads of states and others attacked ordinary citizens. Some acted only in their home town or home region, while others had an international agenda and operated across borders.

So again, terrorism of today is nothing new. Some scholars that have looked into the history of terrorism have tried to find specific characteristics for certain eras or try to discover trends in terrorism. One of them is David Rapoport, he distinguishes four waves in terrorism. Each with its own ingredients, different audiences, sympathizers and supporters, or modus operandi, meaning the way these groups operate. Each of these periods or waves last about a few decades, three or four decades after which they gradually fade out.

The four waves are as follows. The anarchists in the 1880s are the first wave that is followed by an anti-colonial wave from the 1920s on. And this again is followed by a new left wave, what he calls a new left wave. You could also call it the, the red terrorism that started in the 1960s. And then finally, the fourth wave is the religious wave, which according to David Rapoport, started in the year 1979. Let's have a look at each of these waves, starting with the anarchists.

Well, according to David Rapoport that wave started in the 1880s, some say 1870s and it started in Russia. And from there on, it spread to other Parts of the world, Western Europe, America and also Asia. Well its, its founding fathers, you can say, were a number of Russian writers with their doctrine or strategy of terror. Bakunin and Kropotkin were the most famous ones. And they very much used the new technologies, new communication tools of their age, such as the telegraph and mass media in those days, newspapers. One of the most notorious organizations of that era is the Russian organization Narodnaya Volya. the name can best be translated as, the people's will. Well, members of that group killed, amongst others, a Russian tsar and in those days that was definitely breaking news. And according to David Rapoport these People call themselves terrorists and the 1890s has been described as the Golden Age of Assassination. Well it lasted from 1890s on also to the early twentieth century, and some of its victims were the Elizabeth, the Empress of Austria Uberto the first, King of Italy. And a US, a United States President. It was, and here you see a picture of the man President McKinley of the United States who was killed in Buffalo, the state of New York, and this picture is actually one Of the last pictures or the last picture taken of him. The second wave of terrorism that is distinguished by David Rapoport is the wave of the anti-colonialists. What were their main characteristics? Well David Rapoport says it started in the 1920s. And it can be described as a struggle for self-determination, for independence, to liberate certain parts of the world. Former, well now, now former colonies from their occupiers, French rule, British rule, etc. And the tactics these groups used were different from those in the previous wave and they used guerrilla tactics which was difficult for the powers, the British Empire, the French to deal with hit and run tactics. And some of these groups were quite successful in managing to, well almost defeat their opposing forces. Also very important is that, according to David Rapoport, these rebels stopped calling themselves terrorists and were beginning to use the term freedom fighters. So, they were not terrorists. The terrorists were the other party. and they were fighting, they were struggling against what they would call government terror. Among the most well-known organizations of that wave are the IRA. The Irish Republican Army who from the 1920s on and a little bit earlier was fighting for an independent, a free Irish state and also a united one. And then another group that is linked to This anti-colonial wave is the FLN, the Front de Libération Nationale a group of Algerians who managed in the end to fight for an independent Algeria, who were fighting French rule. And then the third organization is Irgun, a militant Zionist group that was fighting the British authorities who at that time were governing what we now call Israel and Palestine

Definition

The <u>definition of terrorism</u> has proved controversial. Various legal systems and government agencies use different <u>definitions of</u>

terrorism in their national legislation. Moreover, the international community has been slow to formulate a universally agreed, legally binding definition of this crime. These difficulties arise from the fact that the term "terrorism" is politically and emotionally charged.[18] In this regard, Angus Martyn, briefing the Australian Parliament, stated that

"The international community has never succeeded in developing an accepted comprehensive definition of terrorism. During the 1970s and 1980s, the United Nations attempts to define the term floundered mainly due to differences of opinion between various members about the use of violence in the context of conflicts over national liberation and self-determination."[1]

These divergences have made it impossible for the United Nations to conclude a Comprehensive Convention on International Terrorism that incorporates a single, all-encompassing, legally binding, criminal law definition of terrorism.[19] The international community has adopted a series of sectoral conventions that define and criminalize various types of terrorist activities.

Since 1994, the United Nations General Assembly has repeatedly condemned terrorist acts using the following political description of terrorism:

"Criminal acts intended or calculated to provoke a state of terror in the general public, a group of persons or particular persons for political purposes are in any circumstance unjustifiable, whatever the considerations of a political, philosophical, ideological, racial, ethnic, religious or any other nature that may be invoked to justify them."[20]

Bruce Hoffman, a scholar, has noted:

It is not only individual agencies within the same governmental apparatus that cannot agree on a single definition of terrorism. Experts and other long-established scholars in the field are equally incapable of reaching a consensus. In the first edition of his magisterial survey, 'Political Terrorism: A Research Guide,' Alex Schmid devoted more than a hundred pages to examining more than a hundred different definitions of terrorism in an effort to discover a broadly acceptable, reasonably comprehensive explication of the word. Four years and a second edition later, Schimd was no closer to the goal of his quest, conceding in the first sentence of the revised volume that the "search for an adequate definition is still on" Walter Laqueur despaired of defining terrorism in both editions of his monumental work on the subject, maintaining that it is neither possible to do so nor worthwhile to make the attempt."[21]

Hoffman believes it is possible to identify some key characteristics of terrorism. He proposes that:

The Baghdad bus station was the scene of a triple car bombing in August 2005 that killed 43 people.

By distinguishing terrorists from other types of criminals and terrorism from other forms of crime, we come to appreciate that terrorism is :

- ineluctably political in aims and motives
- violent – or, equally important, threatens violence
- designed to have far-reaching psychological repercussions beyond the immediate victim or target
- conducted by an organization with an identifiable chain of command or conspiratorial cell structure (whose members wear no uniform or identifying insignia) and
- perpetrated by a subnational group or non-state entity.[22]

A definition proposed by Carsten Bockstette at the George C. Marshall Center for European Security Studies, underlines the psychological and tactical aspects of terrorism:

Terrorism is defined as political violence in an asymmetrical conflict that is designed to induce terror and psychic fear (sometimes indiscriminate) through the violent victimization and destruction of noncombatant targets (sometimes iconic symbols). Such acts are meant to send a message from an illicit clandestine organization. The purpose of terrorism is to exploit the media in order to achieve maximum attainable publicity as an amplifying force multiplier in order to influence the targeted audience(s) in order to reach short- and midterm political goals and/or desired long-term end states."[23]

Oslo, Norway immediately after the 2011 terrorist attack in Norway perpetrated by Anders Behring Breivik.

Walter Laqueur, of the Center for Strategic and International Studies, noted that "the only general characteristic of terrorism generally agreed upon is that terrorism involves violence and the threat of violence".[*citation needed*] This criterion alone does not produce, however, a useful definition, since it includes many violent acts not usually considered terrorism: war, riot, organized crime, or even a simple assault.[*citation needed*] Property destruction that does not endanger life is not usually considered a violent crime.[*according to whom?*] but some have described property destruction by the Earth Liberation Front[24] and Animal Liberation Front[25] as violence and terrorism; see eco-terrorism.

Terrorist attacks are usually carried out in such a way as to maximize the severity and length of the psychological impact.[26] Each act of terrorism is a "performance" devised to have an impact on many large audiences. Terrorists also attack national symbols,[27] to show power and to attempt to shake the foundation of the country or society they are opposed to. This may negatively affect a government, while increasing the prestige of the given terrorist organization and/or ideology behind a terrorist act.[28]

Terrorist acts frequently have a political purpose.[29] Terrorism is a political tactic, like letter-writing or protesting, which is used by activists when they believe that no other means will effect the kind of change they desire.[according to whom?] The change is desired so badly that failure to achieve change is seen as a worse outcome than the deaths of civilians.[citation needed] This is often where the inter-relationship between terrorism and religion occurs. When a political struggle is integrated into the framework of a religious or "cosmic"[30] struggle, such as over the control of an ancestral homeland or holy site such as Israel and Jerusalem, failing in the political goal (nationalism) becomes equated with spiritual failure, which, for the highly committed, is worse than their own death or the deaths of innocent civilians.[31]

Very often, the victims of terrorism are targeted not because they are threats, but because they are specific "symbols, tools, animals or corrupt beings"[citation needed] that tie into a specific view of the world that the terrorists possess. Their suffering accomplishes the terrorists' goals of instilling fear, getting their message out to an audience or otherwise satisfying the demands of their often radical religious and political agendas.[32]

A collection of photographs of those killed during the terrorist attacks on September 11, 2001.

Some official, governmental definitions of terrorism use the criterion of the illegitimacy or unlawfulness of the act.[33][better source needed] to distinguish between actions authorized by a government (and thus "lawful") and those of other actors, including individuals and small groups. Using this criterion, actions that would otherwise qualify as terrorism would not be considered terrorism if they were government sanctioned.[citation needed] For example, firebombing a city, which is designed to affect civilian support for a cause, would not be considered terrorism if it were authorized by a government.[*original research?*] This criterion is inherently problematic and is not universally accepted,[*attribution needed*] because: it denies the existence of state terrorism;[34] the same act may or may not be classed as terrorism depending on whether its sponsorship is traced to a "legitimate" government; "legitimacy" and "lawfulness" are subjective, depending on the perspective of one government or another; and it diverges from the historically accepted meaning and origin of the term.[10][35][36][37]

Among the various definitions there are several that do not recognize the possibility of legitimate use of violence by civilians against an invader in an occupied country.[*citation needed*] Other definitions would label as terrorist groups only the resistance movements that oppose an invader with violent acts that undiscriminately kill or harm civilians and non-combatants, thus making a distinction between lawful and unlawful use of violence.[*citation needed*] According to Ali Khan, the distinction lies ultimately in a political judgment.[38]

An associated, and arguably more easily definable, but *not equivalent* term is violent non-state actor.[39] The semantic scope of this term includes not only "terrorists", but while excluding some individuals or groups who have previously been described as "terrorists", and also explicitly excludes state terrorism. According to the FBI, terrorism is the unlawful use of force or violence against persons or property to intimidate or coerce a government, the civilian population, or any segment thereof, in furtherance of political or social objectives.[*citation needed*]

Barack Obama, commenting on the Boston Marathon bombings of April, 2013, declared "Anytime bombs are used to target innocent civilians, it is an act of terror."[40] Various commentators have pointed out the distinction between "act of terror" and "terrorism", particularly when used by the White House.[41][42][43]

Pejorative use[edit]

The terms "terrorism" and **"terrorist"** (someone who engages in terrorism) carry strong negative connotations.[44] These terms are often used as political labels, to condemn violence or the threat of violence by certain actors as immoral, indiscriminate, unjustified or to condemn an entire segment of a population.[45] Those labeled "terrorists" by their opponents rarely identify themselves as such, and typically use other terms or terms specific to their situation, such as separatist, freedom fighter, liberator, revolutionary, vigilante, militant, paramilitary, guerrilla, rebel, patriot, or any similar-meaning word in other languages and cultures. Jihadi, mujaheddin, and fedayeen are similar Arabic words which have entered the English lexicon. It is common for both parties in a conflict to describe each other as terrorists.[46]

On the question of whether particular terrorist acts, such as killing civilians, can be justified as the lesser evil in a particular circumstance, philosophers have expressed different views: while, according to David Rodin, <u>utilitarian</u> philosophers can (in theory) conceive of cases in which the evil of terrorism is outweighed by the good which could not be achieved in a less morally costly way, in practice the "harmful effects of undermining the convention of non-combatant immunity is thought to outweigh the goods that may be achieved by particular acts of terrorism".[47] Among the non-utilitarian philosophers, <u>Michael Walzer</u> argued that terrorism can be morally justified in only one specific case: when "a nation or community faces the extreme threat of complete destruction and the only way it can preserve itself is by intentionally targeting non-combatants, then it is morally entitled to do so"

In his book *Inside Terrorism* <u>Bruce Hoffman</u> offered an explanation of why the term *terrorism* becomes distorted:

On one point, at least, everyone agrees: *terrorism* is a pejorative term. It is a word with intrinsically negative connotations that is generally applied to one's enemies and opponents, or to those with whom one disagrees and would otherwise prefer to ignore. 'What is called terrorism,' <u>Brian Jenkins</u> has written, 'thus seems to depend on one's point of view. Use of the term implies a moral judgment;

and if one party can successfully attach the label *terrorist* to its opponent, then it has indirectly persuaded others to adopt its moral viewpoint.' Hence the decision to call someone or label some organization *terrorist* becomes almost unavoidably subjective, depending largely on whether one sympathizes with or opposes the person/group/cause concerned. If one identifies with the victim of the violence, for example, then the act is terrorism. If, however, one identifies with the perpetrator, the violent act is regarded in a more sympathetic, if not positive (or, at the worst, an ambivalent) light; and it is not terrorism.[49][50][51]

The pejorative connotations of the word can be summed up in the aphorism, "One man's terrorist is another man's freedom fighter".[46] This is exemplified when a group using irregular military methods is an ally of a state against a mutual enemy, but later falls out with the state and starts to use those methods against its former ally. During World War II, the Malayan People's Anti-Japanese Army was allied with the British, but during the Malayan Emergency, members of its successor (the Malayan Races Liberation Army), were branded "terrorists" by the British.[52][53]More recently, Ronald Reagan and others in the American administration frequently called the Afghan Mujahideen "freedom fighters" during their war against the Soviet Union,[54] yet twenty years later, when a new generation of Afghan men are fighting against what they perceive to be a regime installed by foreign powers, their attacks were labelled "terrorism" by George W. Bush.[55][56][57]Groups accused of terrorism understandably prefer terms reflecting legitimate military or ideological action.[58][59][60] Leading terrorism researcher Professor Martin Rudner, director of the Canadian Centre of Intelligence and Security Studies at Ottawa's Carleton University, defines "terrorist acts" as attacks against civilians for political or other ideological goals, and said:

There is the famous statement: 'One man's terrorist is another man's freedom fighter.' But that is grossly misleading. It assesses the validity of the cause when terrorism is an act. One can have a perfectly beautiful cause and yet if one commits terrorist acts, it is terrorism regardless.[61]

Some groups, when involved in a "liberation" struggle, have been called "terrorists" by the Western governments or media. Later, these same persons, as leaders of the liberated nations, are called "statesmen" by similar organizations. Two examples of this phenomenon are the Nobel Peace Prize laureates Menachem Begin and Nelson Mandela.[62][63][64][65][66][67] WikiLeaks whistleblower Julian Assange has been called a "terrorist" by Sarah Palin and Joe Biden.[68][69]

Sometimes, states which are close allies, for reasons of history, culture and politics, can disagree over whether or not members of a certain organization are terrorists. For instance, for many years, some branches of the United States government refused to label members of the Provisional Irish Republican Army (IRA) as terrorists while the IRA was using methods against one of the United States' closest allies (the United Kingdom) which the UK branded as terrorism. This was highlighted by the Quinn v. Robinson case.[70][71]

For these and other reasons, media outlets wishing to preserve a reputation for impartiality try to be careful in their use of the term.

Types of terrorism

In early 1975, the Law Enforcement Assistant Administration in the United States formed the National Advisory Committee on Criminal Justice Standards and Goals. One of the five volumes that the committee wrote was entitled *Disorders and Terrorism*, produced by the Task Force on Disorders and Terrorism under the direction of H.H.A. Cooper, Director of the Task Force staff.[74] The Task Force classified terrorism into six categories.

- **Civil disorder** – A form of collective violence interfering with the peace, security, and normal functioning of the community.
- **Political terrorism** – Violent criminal behaviour designed primarily to generate fear in the community, or substantial segment of it, for political purposes.
- **Limited political terrorism** – Genuine political terrorism is characterized by a revolutionary approach; limited political terrorism refers to "acts of terrorism which are committed for ideological or political motives but which are not part of a concerted campaign to capture control of the state.
- **Official or state terrorism** – "referring to nations whose rule is based upon fear and oppression that reach similar to terrorism or such proportions." It may also be referred to as **Structural Terrorism** defined broadly as terrorist acts carried out by governments in pursuit of political objectives, often as part of their foreign policy.

Several sources[78][79][80] have further defined the typology of terrorism:

- Political terrorism
  - Sub-state terrorism
    - Social revolutionary terrorism
    - Nationalist-separatist terrorism
    - Religious extremist terrorism
      - Religious fundamentalist Terrorism
      - New religions terrorism
    - Right-wing terrorism
    - Left-wing terrorism
    - Single-issue terrorism
  - State-sponsored terrorism
  - Regime or state terrorism
- Criminal terrorism
- Pathological terrorism

Motivation of terrorists

Attacks on 'collaborators' are used to intimidate people from cooperating with the state in order to undermine state control. This strategy was used in the USA in its War of Independence and in Ireland, in Kenya, in Algeria and in Cyprus during their independence struggles.

Attacks on high profile symbolic targets are

used to incite counter-terrorism by the state to polarise the population. This strategy was used by Al Qaeda in its attacks on the USA in September 2001. These attacks are also used to draw international attention to struggles which are otherwise unreported such as the Palestinian airplane hijackings in 1970 and the South Moluccan hostage crises in the Netherlands in 1975.

Abrahm suggests that terrorist organizations do not select terrorism for its political effectiveness.[81] Individual terrorists tend to be motivated more by a desire for social solidarity with other members of their organization than by political platforms or strategic objectives, which are often murky and undefined.[81]

Democracy and domestic terrorism

Demonstration in Madrid against ETA, January 2000. Roughly a million people met there.

The relationship between domestic terrorism and democracy is very complex. Terrorism is most common in nations with intermediate political freedom, and is least common in the most democratic nations.[82][83][84][85] However, one study suggests that suicide terrorism may be an exception to this general rule. Evidence regarding this particular method of terrorism reveals that every modern suicide campaign has targeted a democracy–a state with a considerable degree of political freedom.[86] The study suggests that concessions awarded to terrorists during the 1980s and 1990s for suicide attacks increased their frequency.[87]

Some examples of "terrorism" in non-democracies include ETA in Spain under Francisco Franco (although the group's terrorist activities increased sharply after Franco's death),[88] the Shining Path in Peru under Alberto Fujimori,[89] the Kurdistan Workers Party when Turkey was ruled by military leaders and the ANC in South Africa.[90] Democracies, such as the United Kingdom, United States, Israel, Indonesia, India, Spain and the Philippines, have also experienced domestic terrorism.

While a democratic nation espousing civil liberties may claim a sense of higher moral ground than other regimes, an act of terrorism within such a state may cause a dilemma: whether to maintain its civil liberties and thus risk being perceived as ineffective in dealing with the problem; or alternatively to restrict its civil liberties and thus risk delegitimizing its claim of supporting civil liberties.[91] For this reason, homegrown terrorism has started to be seen as a greater threat, as stated by former CIA Director Michael Hayden.[92] This dilemma, some social theorists would conclude, may very well play into the initial plans of the acting terrorist(s); namely, to delegitimize the state.[93]

Religious terrorism

Civilians trapped in a London Underground train after a bomb exploded further down the train at Russell Square Tube station on 7th July 2005

Religious terrorism is terrorism performed by groups or individuals, the motivation of which is typically rooted in faith-based tenets. Terrorist acts throughout the centuries have been performed on religious grounds with the hope to either spread or enforce a system of belief, viewpoint or opinion.[95] Religious terrorism does not in itself necessarily define a specific religious standpoint or view, but instead usually defines an individual or a group view or interpretation of that belief system's teachings.

Perpetrators[edit]

The perpetrators of acts of terrorism can be individuals, groups, or states. According to some definitions, clandestine or semi-clandestine state actors may also carry out terrorist acts outside the framework of a state of war. However, the most common image of terrorism is that it is carried out by small and secretive cells, highly motivated to serve a particular cause and many of the most deadly operations in recent times, such as the September 11 attacks, the London underground bombing, and the 2002 Bali bombing were planned and carried out by a close clique, composed of close friends, family members and other strong social networks. These groups benefited from the free flow of information and efficient telecommunications to succeed where others had failed.[96]

Over the years, many people have attempted to come up with a terrorist profile to attempt to explain these individuals' actions through their psychology and social circumstances. Others, like

Roderick Hindery, have sought to discern profiles in the propaganda tactics used by terrorists. Some security organizations designate these groups as *violent non-state actors*.[97] A 2007 study by economist Alan B. Krueger found that terrorists were less likely to come from an impoverished background (28% vs. 33%) and more likely to have at least a high-school education (47% vs. 38%). Another analysis found only 16% of terrorists came from impoverished families, vs. 30% of male Palestinians, and over 60% had gone beyond high school, vs. 15% of the populace.[98]

To avoid detection, a terrorist will look, dress, and behave normally until executing the assigned mission. Some claim that attempts to profile terrorists based on personality, physical, or sociological traits are not useful.[99] The physical and behavioral description of the terrorist could describe almost any normal person.[100] However, the majority of terrorist attacks are carried out by military age men, aged 16–40.[100]

Non-state groups

There is speculation that anthrax mailed inside letters to U.S. politicians was the work of a *lone wolf*.

Main articles: List of designated terrorist organizations and Lone wolf (terrorism)

Groups not part of the state apparatus of in opposition to the state are most commonly referred to as a "terrorist" in the media.

State sponsors[edit]

Main article: *State-sponsored terrorism*

A state can sponsor terrorism by funding or harboring a terrorist organization. Opinions as to which acts of violence by states consist of state-sponsored terrorism vary widely. When states provide funding for groups considered by some to be terrorist, they rarely acknowledge them as such.

State terrorism[edit]

Main article: *State terrorism*

Civilization is based on a clearly defined and widely accepted yet often unarticulated hierarchy. Violence done by those higher on the hierarchy to those lower is nearly always invisible, that is, unnoticed. When it is noticed, it is fully rationalized. Violence done by those lower on the hierarchy to those higher is unthinkable, and when it does occur is regarded with shock, horror, and the fetishization of the victims.

—Derrick Jensen[101]

This terrified baby was almost the only human being left alive in Shanghai's South Station after brutal Japanese bombing, August 28, 1937

As with "terrorism" the concept of "state terrorism" is controversial.[102] The Chairman of the United Nations Counter-Terrorism Committee has stated that the Committee was conscious of 12 international Conventions on the subject, and none of them referred to State terrorism, which was not an international legal concept. If States abused their power, they should be judged against international conventions dealing with war crimes, international human rights and international humanitarian law.[103] Former United Nations Secretary-General Kofi Annan has said that it is "time to set aside debates on so-called 'state terrorism'. The use of force by states is already thoroughly regulated under international law".[104] However, he also made clear that, "regardless of the differences between governments on the question of definition of terrorism, what is clear and what we can all agree on is any deliberate attack on innocent civilians, regardless of one's cause, is unacceptable and fits into the definition of terrorism."[105]

State terrorism has been used to refer to terrorist acts by governmental agents or forces. This involves the use of state resources employed by a state's foreign policies, such as using its military to directly perform acts of terrorism. Professor of Political Science Michael Stohl cites the examples that include Germany's bombing of London and the U.S. atomic destruction of Hiroshima during World War II. He argues that "the use of terror tactics is common in international relations and the state has been and remains a more likely employer of terrorism within the international system than insurgents." They also cite the First strike option as an example of the "terror of coercive diplomacy" as a form of this, which holds the world hostage with the implied threat of using nuclear weapons in "crisis management." They argue that the institutionalized form of terrorism has occurred as a result of changes that took place following World War II. In this analysis, state terrorism exhibited as a form of foreign policy was shaped by the presence and use of weapons of mass destruction, and that the legitimizing of such violent behavior led to an increasingly accepted form of this state behavior.[106][107][107]

Some theorists suggest genocide is a type of terrorism as committed by Adolf Hitler.[citation needed]

State terrorism has also been used to describe peacetime actions by governmental agents such as the bombing of Pan Am Flight 103.[108] Charles Stewart Parnell described William Ewart Gladstone's Irish Coercion Act as terrorism in his "no-Rent manifesto" in 1881, during the Irish Land War.[109] The concept is also used to describe political repressions by governments against their own civilian population with the purpose to incite fear. For example, taking and executing civilian hostages or extrajudicial elimination campaigns are commonly considered "terror" or terrorism, for example during the Red Terror or Great Terror.[110] Such actions are often also described as democide or genocide which has been argued to be equivalent to state terrorism.[111] Empirical studies on this have found that democracies have little democide.[112][113]

Funding[edit]

Main article: Terrorist financing

State sponsors have constituted a major form of funding; for example, Palestine Liberation Organization, Democratic Front for the Liberation of Palestine and some other terrorist groups were funded by the Soviet Union.[114][115] The Stern Gang received funding from Italian Fascist officers in Beirut to undermine the British Mandate for Palestine.[116] Pakistan has created and nurtured terrorist groups as policy for achieving tactical objectives against its neighbours, especially India.[117]

"Revolutionary tax" is another major form of funding, and essentially a euphemism for "protection money".[114] Revolutionary taxes are typically extorted from businesses, and they also "play a secondary role as one other means of intimidating the target population".[114]

Other major sources of funding include

kidnapping for ransoms, smuggling, fraud and robbery.[114]

The Financial Action Task Force is an inter-governmental body whose mandate, since October 2001, has included combatting terrorist financing.[118]

Tactics[edit]

Main article: Tactics of terrorism

The Wall Street bombing at noon on September 16, 1920 killed thirty-eight people and injured several hundred. The perpetrators were never caught.

Terrorism is a form of asymmetric warfare, and is more common when direct conventional warfare will not be effective because forces vary greatly in power.[119]

The context in which terrorist tactics are used is often a large-scale, unresolved political conflict. The type of conflict varies widely; historical examples include:

- Secession of a territory to form a new sovereign state or become part of a different state
- Dominance of territory or resources by various ethnic groups

- Imposition of a particular form of government
- Economic deprivation of a population
- Opposition to a domestic government or occupying army
- Religious fanaticism

Terrorist attacks are often targeted to maximize fear and publicity, usually using explosives or poison.[120] There is concern about terrorist attacks employing weapons of mass destruction. Terrorist organizations usually methodically plan attacks in advance, and may train participants, plant undercover agents, and raise money from supporters or through organized crime. Communications occur through modern telecommunications, or through old-fashioned methods such as couriers.

Responses[edit]

X-ray backscatter technology (AIT) machine used by the TSA to screen passengers. According to the TSA, this is what the remote TSA agent would see on their screen.

Responses to terrorism are broad in scope. They can include re-alignments of the political spectrum and reassessments of fundamental values.

Specific types of responses include:

- Targeted laws, criminal procedures, deportations, and enhanced police powers
- Target hardening, such as locking doors or adding traffic barriers
- Preemptive or reactive military action
- Increased intelligence and surveillance activities
- Preemptive humanitarian activities
- More permissive interrogation and detention policies

The term "counter-terrorism" has a narrower connotation, implying that it is directed at terrorist actors.

According to a report by Dana Priest and William M. Arkin in the Washington Post, "Some 1,271 government organizations and 1,931 private companies work on programs related to counterterrorism, homeland security and intelligence in about 10,000 locations across the United States."[121]

Mass media[edit]

Mass media exposure may be a primary goal of those carrying out terrorism, to expose issues that would otherwise be ignored by the media. Some consider this to be manipulation and exploitation of the media.[122]

The Internet has created a new channel for groups to spread their messages. This has created a cycle of measures and counter measures by groups in support of and in opposition to terrorist movements. The United Nations has created its own online counter-terrorism resource.[123]

The mass media will, on occasion, censor organizations involved in terrorism (through self-restraint or regulation) to discourage further terrorism. However, this may encourage organizations to perform more extreme acts of terrorism to be shown in the mass media. Conversely James F. Pastor explains the significant relationship between terrorism and the media, and the underlying benefit each receives from the other.[124]

There is always a point at which the terrorist ceases to manipulate the media gestalt. A point at which the violence may well escalate, but beyond which the terrorist has become symptomatic of the media gestalt itself. Terrorism as we ordinarily understand it is innately media-related.

—Novelist William Gibson[125]

History[edit]

Main article: History of terrorism

Number of terrorist incidents 2010

The history of terrorism goes back to the Sicarii Zealots, a Jewish extremist group active in Judaea Province at the beginning of the 1st century AD. After Zealotry rebellion in the 1st century AD, when some prominent collaborators with Roman rule were killed,[126][127] according to contemporary historian Josephus, in 6 AD Judas of Galilee formed a small and more extreme offshoot of the Zealots, the Sicarii.[128] Their terror also was directed against Jewish "collaborators", including temple priests, Sadducees, Herodians, and other wealthy elites.[129]

The term "terrorism" itself was originally used to describe the actions of the Jacobin Club during the "Reign of Terror" in the French Revolution. "Terror is nothing other than justice, prompt, severe, inflexible," said Jacobin leader Maximilien Robespierre. In 1795, Edmund Burke denounced the Jacobins for letting "thousands of those hell-hounds called Terrorists ... loose on the people" of France.[130]

In January 1858, Italian patriot Felice Orsini threw three bombs in an attempt to assassinate French Emperor Napoleon III.[131] Eight bystanders were killed and 142 injured.[131] The incident played a crucial role as an inspiration for the development of the early Russian terrorist groups.[131] Russian Sergey Nechayev, who founded People's Retribution in 1869, described himself as a "terrorist", an early example of the term being employed in its modern meaning.[15] Nechayev's story is told in fictionalized form by Fyodor Dostoevsky in the novel *The Possessed*. German anarchist writer Johann Most dispensed "advice for terrorists" in the 1880s.[132]

One of the key problems when researching terrorism is the secretive nature of terrorists and terrorism, they work in the dark, underground, it's very difficult to study them. Well, this challenge is also a challenge to policymakers. They would like to know who they're dealing with, and they would like to discover terrorists before they strike. And a phrase that is connected to that need and challenge is the following, looking for the needle in the haystack. Well that sounds like a mission impossible, you can't find a needle in a haystack. But fortunately, there have been quite a Few cases of terrorists that have been caught before they managed to strike and some have been caught afterwards based on certain clues or signs. So apparently it's not impossible to find them. And perhaps they are recognizable. Perhaps it is possible to make a distinction between terrorists on the one hand and non-terrorists on the other, and to find terrorists out of a larger population of non-terrorists.

Well the process or tool to do so is called profiling. How does it work? Profiling goes under different names, Including its original, criminal or offender profiling. And there are different types of profiling. The main distinction is that between a focus on the individual characteristics of a person, versus a focus on their behavior. So personality profiling versus behavioral profiling. And the most prevalent method of attempting to achieve a distinction between an offender, either a criminal or a terrorist, and a non-offender is to establish a set of psychological, socio-economic, physical, behavioral, and or ethnic attributes based on prior experiences. Well, in other words, indicators that tell us what a terrorist might look like, what are its behavioral or personality traits, and in what circumstances do they live and work, all together making up the terrorist profile. And oftentimes, this is followed by data mining or data searching, using various sources for what is called secondary security screening of the group of individuals with the largest number of indicators.

So it's two steps. First, you look at the population as a whole, then you have a group that have quite a number of indicators, and then you're, you are going to do some data mining, data searching, trying to and hopefully getting out of it, a number of people that might be terrorists or, ideally, that are the terrorists. Well, if it works. In an ideal situation, it might offer the counter-terrorism agencies a perfect tool to discover terrorists without much prior information about this individual or group, purely based on past experiences, past experience with other groups or individuals. Obviously there's a demand for a tool that could really do this. Terrorist attacks cost a lot of casualties and property damage, and counter-terrorism measures have an impact on the lives of many and also cost a lot.

Well here's a, a statement that is a good example of the demand for a tool, a mechanism to make a distinction between terrorists and non-terrorists. And it's a statement from a, a newspaper in Germany that was published in December 2010, and it said airports demand racial profiling to fight terror. And it reads, the incoming head of Germany's main airport lobby group is Demanding the nation's transit authorities use racial profiling to weed out terrorists at security checks. Well, the idea is that it does not only make travelling safer but it also reduce costs. If you use your resources to try to scan and assess everyone you're wasting a lot of money a lot of time as well that could also be used on other precautionary measures. So, any tool that could help us to speed up that process

m

Chapter 5
Armed Conflict

18 Alert 2010

Countries engaged in armed conflicts (indicator no. 1) Ending of armed conflict during 2009 Armed Conflicts **19**

This chapter analyzes the armed conflicts that took place during 2009 (indicator 1). The chapter has two main sections,

apart from the definition that follows and the map at the beginning which shows the active conflicts in 2009.

The first section contains an analysis of the

global trends in armed conflicts in 2009 and the second describes the
evolution and most notable events of each armed conflict during the year.

1.1. Armed conflicts: definition

An **armed conflict** is any confrontation between regular or irregular armed groups with objectives that are perceived as incompatible and where the continuous and organized use of violence: a) causes a minimum of 100 battle-related
deaths in a year and/or has a serious impact on the territory (e.g. destruction of infrastructures or natural resources)
and the human security (e.g. injury or displacement of civilians, sexual violence, food insecurity, effect on mental
health and the social fabric or interruption of basic services); b) pursues goals that can be differentiated from common
crime and are normally linked to:
- demands for self-determination and self government, or identity issues;
- opposition to the political, economic, social or

ideological system of a State or the internal or international policies
of the government, which in both cases produces a struggle to take or erode power;
- or to control the resources or the territory.

A. ARMED CONFLICT AS THE TRIGGER

The concurrent application of international human rights and humanitarian law can happen only when a series of objective conditions are met. International humanitarian law being essentially a body of law applicable to armed conflict, the existence of a situation amounting to an armed conflict is necessary to trigger its applicability in conjunction with international human rights law. The next sections will address the question of what an armed conflict is and what types of armed conflict international humanitarian law applies to. It should, however, be noted that a number of international humanitarian law obligations require action before a conflict begins or after a conflict ends. For example, States must provide training in international humanitarian law to their armed forces in order to prevent potential abuse; States must also encourage the teaching of international humanitarian law to the civilian population; domestic legislation must be adopted implementing its relevant provisions, including the obligation to include war crimes in domestic law; States must also prosecute persons who have committed war crimes. One category of war crimes, grave breaches of the Geneva Conventions and of Protocol I, must be prosecuted according to the principle of universal jurisdiction, i.e., independently of where the crime has been committed and of the nationality of the offender and of the victims. Thus, some violations of international humanitarian law could be established and their perpetrators punished outside the time frame and the geographical context of an actual armed conflict.

The concurrent applicability of international human rights and humanitarian law depends on the objective legal conditions required for the corresponding legal norms to apply. In this particular case of the relationship between international human rights law and international humanitarian law, it is the existence of an armed conflict that will trigger the application of the latter and, thus, of the complementary application of international human rights and international humanitarian protections. The following sections will discuss the different types of conflict as defined in conventional and customary international law and will also analyse the challenges posed by certain uses of force that do not reach the threshold of an armed conflict.

1. nternational armed conflict

Article 2 common to the Geneva Conventions states that "[i]n addition to the provisions which shall be implemented in peacetime, the present

Convention shall apply to all cases of declared war or of any other armed conflict which may arise between two or more of the High Contracting Parties, even if the state of war is not recognized by one of them. The Convention shall also apply to all cases of partial or total occupation of the territory of a High Contracting Party, even if the said occupation meets with no armed resistance." Protocol I to the Geneva Conventions extends the situations covered by common article 2, stating that the situations to which the Protocol applies "include armed conflicts in which peoples are fighting against colonial domination and alien occupation and against racist regimes in the exercise of their right of self-determination" (art. 1.4).

While the Geneva Conventions and Protocol I indicate the type of situations to which they will apply, they do not provide a clear definition of "armed conflict". The existence of an armed conflict is a precondition for the application of international humanitarian law, but the existing body of rules is not clear about the elements necessary to determine that a situation between two States has reached the threshold of an armed conflict. Indeed, common article 2 limits the scope of the Geneva Conventions to conflicts in which one or more States have recourse to armed force against another State. The commentary to the Geneva Conventions provides further guidance when it indicates that "any difference arising between two States and leading to the intervention of members of the armed forces is an armed conflict within the meaning of article 2, even if one of the Parties denies the existence of a state of war. It makes no difference how long the conflict lasts, or how much slaughter takes place."34 Furthermore, the International Criminal Tribunal for the former Yugoslavia has stated that "an armed conflict exists whenever there is a resort to armed force between States".35

One of the problems of the lack of a clear definition is that, for example, it is uncertain whether international humanitarian law would apply in low-intensity military confrontation, such as border incidents or armed skirmishes. International law does not provide guidance on the precise meaning of "use of force" or "armed conflict" in the context of the Charter of the United Nations and of the Geneva Conventions. While some claim that every act of armed violence between two States is covered by international humanitarian law of international armed conflicts, others consider that a threshold of intensity should be applied.36

Notwithstanding this lack of clarity, it is important to remember that, irrespective of the existence of an actual armed conflict, international human rights law continues to apply. As the hostilities unfold, international humanitarian law will be triggered and its protections and standards will complement, complete and in certain cases further clarify international human rights protections, guarantees and minimum standards.

34 Jean Pictet et al., eds., *Geneva Convention I for the Amelioration of the Condition of the Wounded and Sick in Armed Forces in the Field: Commentary* (Geneva, ICRC, 1952), p. 32.

35 *Prosecutor* v. *Duško Tadi'c*, case No. IT-94-1-A, Decision on the defence motion for interlocutory appeal on jurisdiction, 2 October 1995, para. 70.

36 See, in this respect, the International Criminal Tribunal for the former Yugoslavia's decision on Tadi'c's defence motion for interlocutory appeal on jurisdiction, where the Appeals Chamber indicates that hostilities in the former Yugoslavia in 1991 and 1992 "exceed the intensity requirements applicable to both international and internal armed conflicts." Ibid.

2. Non-international armed conflict

International humanitarian law contains two different legal frameworks dealing with non-international armed conflicts. On the one hand, article 3 common to the Geneva Conventions stipulates that "in the case of armed conflict not of an international character" a series of minimum provisions of international humanitarian law shall apply.37 The Conventions do not define what "non-international armed conflict" means, but it is now commonly accepted that it refers to armed confrontations between the armed forces of a State and non-governmental armed groups or between non-State armed groups.38 Protocol II to the Geneva Conventions provides that the Protocol applies to armed conflicts "which take place in the territory of a High Contracting Party between its armed forces and dissident armed forces or other organized armed groups which, under responsible command, exercise such control over a part of its territory as to enable them to carry out sustained and concerted military operations and to implement this Protocol" (art. 1).

The International Criminal Tribunal for the former Yugoslavia's Appeals Chamber has indicated that an armed conflict exists whenever there is protracted armed violence between governmental authorities and organized armed groups or between such groups within a State. It has

37 According to common article 3, these minimum guarantees are: "(1) Persons taking no active part in the hostilities, including members of armed forces who have laid down their arms and those placed hors de combat by sickness, wounds, detention, or any other cause, shall in all circumstances be treated humanely, without any adverse distinction founded on race, colour, religion or faith, sex, birth or wealth, or any other similar criteria. To this end, the following acts are and shall remain prohibited at any time and in any place whatsoever with respect to the above-

mentioned persons: (a) violence to life and person, in particular murder of all kinds, mutilation, cruel treatment and torture;
(b) taking of hostages; (c) outrages upon personal dignity, in particular humiliating and degrading treatment; (d) the passing of sentences and the carrying out of executions without previous judgement pronounced by a regularly constituted court, affording all the judicial guarantees which are recognized as indispensable by civilized peoples.
(2) The wounded and sick shall be collected and cared for."

38 See ICRC, "How is the term 'armed conflict' defined in international humanitarian law?", Opinion Paper, March 2008.**36 37**

further indicated that international humanitarian law applies from the initiation of such armed conflicts and extends beyond the cessation of hostilities until a peaceful settlement is achieved.39 In the *Haradinaj* case, the Trial Chamber stated that the criterion of protracted armed violence is to be interpreted as referring more to the intensity of the armed violence than to its duration. In addition, armed groups involved must have a minimum degree of organization. The Trial Chamber summarized the indicative factors that the Tribunal has relied on when assessing the two criteria. For assessing the intensity these include "the number, duration and intensity of individual confrontations; the type of weapons and other military equipment used; the number and calibre of munitions fired; the number of persons and type of forces partaking in the fighting; the number of casualties; the extent of material destruction; and the number of civilians fleeing combat zones. The involvement of the [United Nations] Security Council may also be a reflection of the intensity of a conflict." On the degree of organization an armed group must have to make hostilities between that group and governmental forces a non-international armed conflict, the Tribunal has stated that an "armed conflict can exist only between parties that are sufficiently organized to confront each other with military means. [...] [I]ndicative factors include the existence of a command structure and disciplinary rules and mechanisms within the group; the existence of a headquarters; the fact that the group controls a certain territory; the ability of the group to gain access to weapons, other military equipment, recruits and military training; its ability to plan, coordinate and carry out military operations, including troop movements and logistics; its ability to define a unified military strategy and use military tactics; and its ability to speak with one voice and negotiate and conclude agreements such as ceasefire or peace accords."[40]

Similarly, ICRC proposes those two criteria of intensity of violence and organization of non-State parties as determining the lower threshold for

---

39 *Prosecutor* v. *Duško Tadic´*, para. 70.

40 *Prosecutor* v. *Ramush Haradinaj et. al.*, case No. IT-04-84-T, Judgement of 3 April 2008, paras. 49 and 60.

the application of international humanitarian law of non-international armed conflicts:

"First, the hostilities must reach a minimum level of intensity. This may be the case, for example, when the hostilities are of a collective character or when the Government is obliged to use military force against the insurgents, instead of mere police forces;

"Second, non-governmental groups involved in the conflict must be considered as 'parties to the conflict', meaning that they possess organized armed forces. This means for example that these forces have to be under a certain command structure and have the capacity to sustain military operations."[41]

It should be noted that the regulations in Protocol II concerning non-international armed conflicts are narrower than those under common article 3. For example, Protocol II introduces a requirement of territorial control for non-State actors. Furthermore, while Protocol II expressly applies only to armed conflicts between State armed forces and dissident armed forces or other organized armed groups, common article 3 applies also to armed conflicts occurring only between non-State armed groups.42 Moreover, Protocol II requires a command structure for non-State armed groups, which is not expressly included in common article 3.

It can be difficult to establish whether these requirements are met in a particular situation. Determining what constitutes "responsible command" is difficult as the command of an armed group might change over time. Ascertaining the exercise of control over a part of the territory is particularly complex as armed groups rarely maintain a single sustained area of operations, but may move frequently from place to place. It is

41 See ICRC, "How is the term "armed conflict" defined in international humanitarian law?"

42 In this context ICRC has indicated that "Protocol II 'develops and supplements' common article 3 'without modifying its existing

conditions of application'. This means that this restrictive definition is relevant for the application of Protocol II only, but does not extend to the law of [non-international armed conflicts] in general." See ICRC, "How is the term "armed conflict" defined in international humanitarian law?"**38 39**

II. REQUIREMENTS, LIMITATIONS AND EFFECTS OF THE CONCURRENT APPLICABILITY OF INTERNATIONAL HUMAN RIGHTS LAW AND INTERNATIONAL HUMANITARIAN LAW IN ARMED CONFLICT

beyond the scope of this publication to examine the details of practice and jurisprudence on this issue. However, regional and international courts, ICRC and numerous academics have produced opinions that explain in some detail how these criteria may be interpreted. In any case, it should be noted that even if the stricter criteria of Protocol II are not entirely met, a situation may still be covered by common article 3 as international humanitarian law's "minimum guarantee".43 As indicated above, unlike article 1 of Protocol II, common article 3 of the Geneva Conventions does not make the same references to "responsible command", "exercise of control" or "organized armed groups" and, therefore, has a significantly lower threshold of application. Under common article 3, an armed conflict could potentially exist between two armed groups, without any involvement of State forces. Common article 3 is, thus, seen as defining the lowest threshold of armed conflict, below which there is no armed conflict and international humanitarian law is not applicable.

Finally, it is important to recall, as indicated above, that in non-international armed conflicts the intensity of hostilities plays a fundamental role in triggering the application of international humanitarian law and, thus, the concurrent applicability regime. So to distinguish an armed conflict from other forms of violence, such as internal disturbances and tensions, riots or acts of banditry, the situation must reach a certain threshold of confrontation. This question is relevant because, as has already been indicated, the application of international humanitarian law can be triggered only through the existence of an armed conflict. There is, however, no specific organ or authority with special responsibility for determining whether an armed conflict is taking place or not. It is not necessary for

43 The International Court of Justice held that "article 3 which is common to all four Geneva Conventions of 12 August 1949 defines certain rules to be applied in the armed conflicts of a non-international character. There is no doubt that, in the event of international armed conflicts, these rules also constitute a minimum yardstick, in addition to the more elaborate rules which are also to apply to international conflicts; and they are rules which, in the Court's opinion, reflect what the Court in 1949 called 'elementary considerations of humanity'." *Military and Paramilitary Activities in and against Nicaragua (Nicaragua v. United States of America), Merits, Judgment, I.C.J. Reports 1986*, para. 218.

INTERNATIONAL LEGAL PROTECTION OF HUMAN RIGHTS IN ARMED CONFLICT

the parties to a conflict to recognize that actual armed conflict exists. This determination must be made primarily on the basis of the situation on the ground, according to the relevant provisions of international humanitarian law. In addition, public statements by ICRC or the United Nations would be significant in determining that there is an armed conflict.

Why is it important to determine when the applicability of international humanitarian rules has been triggered? International human rights law and international humanitarian law share a number of protections and standards aimed at protecting civilians from the effects of war. Yet, because international humanitarian law gives States more leeway when they use armed force (for example, on the use of deadly force) and, according to certain States, when they detain enemies without judicial procedure (like prisoners of war in international armed conflicts), there may be a temptation to invoke rules of international humanitarian law in a situation where the threshold of armed force has *not* been reached. In those unclear cases it is essential to consider international human rights law as the only applicable legal regime, until such time that the threshold and conditions of an armed conflict have been met.**40**

1. Armed Conflicts
- In 2009 31 armed conflicts were reported, but a decrease in hostilities in Sri Lanka (northeast) and India (Nagaland) meant that at the end of the year 29 conflicts were active. The only addition
to the list of conflicts with respect to 2008 is Sudan (southern).
- The large majority of armed conflicts took place in Asia (14) and Africa (10), while the rest occurred in Europe (three) the Middle East (three) and America (one).
- Approximately two thirds of the armed conflicts in 2009 were linked to identity issues

and demands for greater self-government.
- The highest intensity armed conflicts took place in Afghanistan, Colombia, Iraq, DR Congo (east), Pakistan (northeast), Somalia, Sri Lanka, Sudan (south) and Uganda (north).
- Violence increased in Yemen as part of the conflict between the Government and the followers of al-Houthi, in the north of the country, having a dramatic impact on the civilian population.
- Violence in Afghanistan became worse and in northeast Pakistan, with thousands of deaths, due to the expansion of the Taliban militia and an increase in terrorist attacks and clashes between insurgent groups and security forces.
- In Africa, the LRA area of operations moved from the north of Uganda to the border region between DR Congo, Sudan and the Central African Republic, while Somalia was witness to the

worst escalation of violence in the last 20 years.

Figure 1.1. **Conflict dynamics**

ARMED CONFLICT (War)

Conflict prevention

Escalation of hostilities

Ceasefire Agreement

WAR PHASE

Socio-political crises continue to exist. May be a new prewar phase if not correctly managed

POSTWAR PHASE (OR UNRESOLVED CONFLICTS)

HIGH TENSION (start of direct violence)

UNSTABLE PEACE (start of socio-political crises)

STABLE PEACE

LASTING PEACE

PRE-WAR PHASE

20 Alert 2010

Table 1.1. **Summary of armed conflicts 2009**

Confl ict1

-start date-

Type2 Main parties 3

Intensity4

Trend5

Africa

Algeria

-1992-

Internationalized internal Government, Salafi st Group for Preaching and Combat (GSPC) / al-Qaeda Organization in the Islamic Maghreb (AQIM)

2

System =

Chad

-2006-

Internationalized internal Government, new UFR coalition of armed groups (UFDD, UFDDFundamental,

RFC, CNT, FSR, UFCD, UDC, FPRN), MDJT, FPIR,

Janjaweed militias, Toro Boro militia, Sudan, France

2

Government ?

Ethiopia (Ogaden)

-2007-

Internal

Government, ONLF, OLF, pro-government militias

2

Self-government, Identity =

Nigeria (Niger Delta)

-2001-

Internal Government, MEND, MOSOP, NDPVF and NDV, militias from the Ijaw, Itsekeri, Urhobo and Ogoni communities, private security groups

2

Resources, Identity ?

Central African Rep.

-2006-

Internationalized internal Government, APRD, UFRD, armed groups split from UFDR (FURCA, MJLC), FDPC, France, MICOPAX, EUFOR

RCA/TCHAD and highway bandits (Zaraguinas)
1
Government =
DR Congo (East)
-1998-
Internationalized internal Government, Mai-Mai militias, FDLR, FDLR-RUD, CNDP, FRF, PARECO, APCLS, armed Ituri groups, Burundian FNL armed opposition group,
Ugandan ADF-NALU and LRA armed opposition group, Rwanda,
MONUC
3
Identity, Government, Resources =
Somalia
-1988-
Internationalized internal
New Transitional Federal Government (TFG) – including the moderate
faction of the Alliance for the Reliberation of Somalia (ARS), and
supported by Ahl as-Sunna wal-Jama'a, warlords, Ethiopia, US,

AMISOM–, radical faction of the Alliance for the Reliberation of Somalia (ARS) –including part of the Union of Islamic Courts (UIC), Hizbul Islam, al-Shabab– and supported by Eritrea.

3

Government =

Sudan (South)

-2009-

Internal

Ethnic communities militias, National Unity Government and the Government of South Sudan

3

Territory, Resources, Selfgovernment

?

Sudan (Darfur)

-2003-

Internationalized internal

Government, pro-government Janjaweed militias, JEM, several factions of the SLA and other armed groups

2

Self-government, Resources,

Identity
⍰
Uganda (North)
-1986-
Internationalized internal Armed Forces of Uganda, Central African Republic, DR Congo and from
South Sudan, pro-government militias from DR Congo and from South
Sudan, LRA
3
Self-government, Identity ⍰

America
Colombia
-1964-
Internationalized internal
Government, FARC, ELN, paramilitary groups
3
System =

Asia
Afghanistan
-2001-
Internationalized internal Government, international coalition (led by the US), ISAF

(NATO), Taliban militia, warlords | 3 | System ⁇

Philippines (NPA) -1969- | Internal | Government, NPA | 1 | System =

Philippines (Mindanao-MILF) -1978- | Internal | Government, MILF | 2 | Self-government, Identity ⁇

Philippines (Mindanao-Abu Sayyaf) -1991- | Internationalized internal | Government, Abu Sayyaf | 1 | Self-government, Identity, System ⁇

India (Assam)
-1983-
Internationalized internal
Government, ULFA, DHD, Black Widow, NDFB
2
Self-government, Identity =
Armed Conflicts **21**
1. This column includes those States where armed conflict is taking place and indicates in parenthesis the region within the State where the conflict
is confined or the name of the armed group involved in the conflict. This last option is used in those cases where there is more than one armed conflict in the same State or in the same territory within the State, with the purpose of differentiating them.
2. The report classifies and analyses armed conflicts using a dual typology which addresses, on the one hand, the causes or incompatibility of
interests and, on the other hand, the convergence of the scenario of the conflict and the parties involved. With regard to the main

causes the following can be distinguished: demands for self-determination and self-government (Self-government) or identity issues (Identity); opposition

Conflict -start date-
Type Main parties
Intensity
Trend

Asia

India (Jammu and Kashmir) -1989-
Internationalized internal
Government, JKLF, Lashkar-e-Tayyeba, Hizb-ul-Mujahideen
2
Self-government, Identity ?

India (Manipur) -1982-
Internal
Government, PLA, UNLF, PREPAK, KNF, KNA, KYNL
2

Self-government, Identity ⬜
India (Nagaland)
-1955-
Internal
Government, NSCN-K, NSCN-IM
1
Self-government, Identity End
India (CPI-M)
-1967-
Internal
Government, CPI-M (Naxalites)
2
System ⬜
Myanmar
-1948-
Internal Government, armed groups (KNU, SSA-S, KNPP, UWSA, CNF, ALP, DKBA, KNU/KNLA, KNPLAC, SSNPLO)
1
Self-government, Identity ⬜
Pakistan (Baluchistan)
-2005-
Internal
Government, BLA, BRA and BLF

2
Self-government, Resources =
Pakistan (northwest)
-2001-
Internationalized internal
Government, Taliban militias, tribal militias, US
3
System ?
Sri Lanka (northeast)
-1983-
Internal
Government, LTTE
3
Self-government, Identity End
Thailand (South)
-2004-
Internal
Government, secessionist armed opposition groups
2
Self-government, Identity =

Europe
Russia (Chechnya)
-1999-

Internal Russian Federal Government, Government of Chechnya, armed opposition groups

1

Self-government, Identity, System ⁇

Russia (Ingushetia)

-2008-

Internal Russian Federal Government, Government of Ingushetia, armed opposition groups (Jamaat Ingush)

1

System ⁇

Turkey (Southeast)

-1984-

Internationalized internal

Government, PKK, TAK

2

Self-government, Identity ⁇

Middle East

Iraq

-2003-

Internationalized internal International coalition led by the USA/ United Kingdom, internal and external armed opposition groups

3
System, Government, Resources =
Israel- Palestine
-2000-
International Israeli government, settlers' militias, PNA, Fatah (Al Aqsa Martyrs Brigades), Hamas (Ezzedin al Qassam Brigades), Islamic Jihad, FPLP,
FDLP, Popular Resistance Committees
2
Self-government, Identity, Territory ⬇
Yemen
-2004-
Internationalized internal
Government, followers of the cleric al-Houthi (al-Shabab al-Mumen)
2
System ⬇

1: Low intensity; 2: Medium intensity; 3: High intensity;
⬆: Escalation of violence; ⬇: Decrease of violence; = : Unchanged; End: No longer considered an armed confl ict

22 Alert 2010

1.2. Armed conflicts: global trends in 2009

In 2009, 31 armed conflicts were reported, although at the end of the year only 29 remained active. During the year the military victory of the Sri Lankan Army over the LTTE and a decline in hostilities in the Indian state of Nagaland meant that both contexts were no longer considered armed conflicts. Compared to 2008, the total number of armed conflicts remains unchanged (31 conflicts during the year, 30 active at the end of the year) and the only variation is the inclusion of Sudan (south), which experienced a serious increase in violence. The large majority of armed conflicts took place in Asia (14) and Africa (10), followed by Europe (3), the

Middle East (3) and America (1). In all of the cases analyzed in this section, the State was one of the contending parties. Nevertheless, in numerous conflicts there were frequent clashes between non-state armed actors, while in other contexts, such as Sudan (south), inter-communal violence explained a considerable part of the high mortality rates. All of the conflicts, except the dispute between Israel and Palestine,6 were internal (14) or internationalized internal (16). The average duration of armed conflicts in 2009 was nearly 18 years, although this figure is questionable due to the difficulty of setting an exact start date for a conflict and due to the high number of current armed conflicts that have been through previous cycles of violence. Although armed conflicts have multiple causes, it should be noted that **almost two out of three conflicts (19 of 31) refer mainly to identity issues or demands for greater self-government**. On the other hand, there are 14 cases where the main divergence is rooted in opposition to a specific Government or to the political, economic, social or ideological system of a State. Of these, there were five cases – Iraq, Chad, Central African Republic, DR Congo (east) and Somalia– where several armed groups were struggling to take power or undermine the

central Government. In those cases where the main reason
for the confl ict is opposition to the State system, we
can identify two categories. In the fi rst, which includes
Colombia, Philippines (NPA) and India (CPI-M), the insurgency
advocates the establishment of a socialist style political and economic system. In the second category,

Graph 1.1. **Regional distribution of the number of armed conflicts**

2 4 6 8 10
America
Middle East
Europe
Africa
Asia
0 12 14 16

to the political, economic, social or ideological system of a State (System) or the internal or international policies of a government (Government),

which in both cases produces a struggle to take or erode power; or control over the resources (Resources) or the territory (Territory). In connection with the second typology, armed conflicts can be internal, internationalised internal or international. Internal armed conflict is any
confrontation involving armed parties from the same State that operate exclusively within its territory. Second, an internationalized internal armed conflict is when some of the adversaries are foreign, and/or when the confrontation extends into a neighbouring country. To consider an
armed conflict as internationalized internal, it is also taken into account the fact that the armed groups have their military bases in neighbouring countries, with the connivance of those States, and launch their attacks from them. Finally, international conflict is taken to be those where state or non-state actors from two or more countries are in conflict. In addition, it must be considered that most of the current armed conflicts

have an important regional and international dimension and influence due to factors such as the flow of refugees, arms trade, economic or political interests (such as the legal or illegal exploitation of resources) that neighbouring countries have in the conflict, the participation of
foreign combatants or logistic and military support provided by other States.

3. The main players that intervene in the conflicts are made up of a mixture of regular or irregular armed actors. The conflicts usually involve the
Government, or its Armed Forces, against one or several armed opposition groups, but can also include other irregular groups such as clans,
guerrillas, warlords, armed groups confronting each other or militias from ethnic or religious communities. Although they most frequently use
conventional weapons, and more specifically small arms (which cause most of the deaths in the conflicts), in many cases other methods

such as suicide attacks, bombings and sexual violence are used; even hunger is employed as a weapon of war.

4. The intensity of an armed conflict (high, medium or low) and its trend (escalation of violence, decrease of violence, unchanged) are evaluated mostly based on how deadly it is (number of fatalities) and other consequences on the population and the territory. In addition, there are other aspects to be considered, such as the systematization and frequency of the violence or the complexity of the military struggle (the complexity is normally related to the number of parties involved and how fragmented they are, the level of institutionalization and the capabilities of the State and the degree of internationalization of the conflict, as well as the flexibility of the objectives and the political willingness of the parties to

reach an agreement). As a consequence, high intensity armed conflicts are usually those that cause over 1,000 annual battle-related deaths and also affect significant parts of the territory and population and include numerous actors (that establish relationships of alliances, confrontation
or tactical coexistence among themselves). Medium and low intensity conflicts, with over 100 annual battle-related deaths, have the aforementioned characteristics but with a more limited presence and scope. An armed conflict is considered to be ended when a significant and
sustained decrease in armed hostilities occurs because of a military victory, agreement between the actors in conflict, demobilization by one of
the parties or because one of the parties abandons the armed struggle or limits it considerably as a strategy to achieve specific objectives. None
of these options necessarily imply that the root causes of the armed conflict have been

overcome or exclude the possibility of new outbreaks of
violence. A temporary halt in hostilities, formal or tacit, does not necessarily entail the end of an armed conflict

5. In this column the evolution of events in the current year (2009) is compared with the previous year (2008). The escalation of violence symbol
(⬆) is shown if the general situation of the conflict during 2009 is worse than the previous year, the reduction of violence symbol (⬇) if things
have improved and the unchanged sign (=) if no significant change has taken place.

6. Although Palestine (whose Palestine National Authority is a political entity linked to a specific population and territory) is not an internationally
recognized State, the conflict between Israel and Palestine is considered "international" and not "internal" since it is a territory which has been illegally occupied and it is not recognized as being part of Israel under International Law

or by a United Nations resolution.

Armed Conflicts 23

some of the contending parties have stated their intention
to create an Islamic State or include essential elements
of Islamic law in the institutions and laws of the State, such as the cases of Algeria, Afghanistan, Philippines
(Mindanao-Abu Sayyaf), Iraq, Pakistan (northeast),
Russia (Chechnya), Russia (Ingushetia), Somalia and Yemen. It should be noted that some of the armed
opposition groups that operate in those countries have
been accused of having ties to the al-Qaeda network.
Apart from the cases where the cause of the confl ict is
linked to identity and self-government or to the type of
government or system, there are several countries where

control of resources and the territory are essential to understanding the origin and the dynamics of the military conflict. This was especially clear in the cases of **Iraq, Nigeria (Niger Delta), Pakistan (Baluchistan), DR Congo (east), Sudan (Darfur) and Sudan (south), although in many other cases the control of, or access to, resources fuelled and aggravated the dispute**. With regard to intensity, **in nine cases – Afghanistan, Colombia, Iraq, DR Congo (east), Pakistan (northwest), Somalia, Sri Lanka, Sudan (south) and Uganda (north)– very high levels of violence caused the death of nearly 1,000 people**, although in some of these cases, such as Afghanistan, Pakistan (northwest), Iraq, Sri Lanka, Somalia or Sudan (south), the number of deaths was much higher. Two countries joined the list of high intensity conflicts compared to the previous year: Uganda (mainly because of the spread of the LRA's armed activities to countries such as Sudan, Central African Republic or DR Congo) and southern Sudan (mostly due to increase in inter-communal violence). In contrast, conflict intensity decreased appreciably in some of the most virulent struggles of 2008, such as Chad, Israel-Palestine and Sudan (Darfur). Similar to last year, most of the armed conflicts were medium intensity (15 conflicts) and the remaining seven cases – India (Nagaland), Philippines (Mindanao-Abu Sayyaf), Philippines (NPA),

Myanmar, Central African Republic, Russia (Chechnya) and Russia (Ingushetia)- were low intensity. If we compare the situation to the previous year, **in 10 of the 29 active confl icts at the end of the year there was an increase in hostilities**, in eleven cases the situation did not change considerably and in eight cases a decrease in violence was reported: Chad, Nigeria (Niger Delta), Sudan (Darfur), Philippines (Mindanao-MILF), India (Jammu and Kashmir), India (Manipur), Turkey (southeast) and Israel- Palestine.

Graph 1.2. **Intensity of the armed conflicts**
Low **23%**
High **29%**
Medium **48%**

Graph 1.3. **Intensity of the conflicts by region**

America
Middle East
Europe
Africa
Asia

0 2 4 6 8

High Medium Low

a) **Regional trends**

By region, it should be noted that **most of the confl icts in Africa are linked to the struggle to take or erode current power due to opposition to the internal or international polices of the Government**. However, the number of confl icts where demands of self-government of a territory or group are the key to the confl ict is much lower than the worldwide average. In fact, although in the cases of DR Congo (east), Nigeria (Niger Delta) and Uganda (north), identity grievances have been used to justify the struggle or mobilize certain sectors of the population, the cases of Ethiopia (Ogaden) and Sudan (south) are the only ones where the issue of self-government plays an important role. The second main feature of the confl icts in Africa is the regional dimension, due to the important role that Governments from neighbouring countries play on many occasions and also because numerous armed groups have their bases in adjacent countries. In this regard, of note is the clear link between the confl icts that are taking place in the Central African Republic, Chad and Sudan (Darfur), the incursions by the

Ethiopian Armed Forces in Somalia to support the Transitional Federal Government, the activity by armed groups from Rwanda in eastern DR Congo or the internationalization of the conflict in northern Uganda caused by the expansion of LRA activities to the southeast of the Central African Republic, northeast DR Congo and southeast Sudan. Except for the cases of Ethiopia (Ogaden), Sudan (south) and Nigeria (Niger Delta), all of the African conflicts were classified as internationalized internal. Another feature of armed conflicts in Africa is the high number of armed actors. Thus, in the cases of DR Congo (east), Somalia, Sudan (Darfur), and Nigeria (Niger Delta) the number of armed actors actively involved in the hostilities is greater than 10, and in another seven cases there are a minimum of four armed actors. Currently, the average duration of armed conflicts in Africa (approximately nine years) is signifi cantly below the world average (18 years) and the average for the rest of the continents. Thus, only three of the nine confl icts – Algeria, Somalia and Uganda (north)– have been going on for over 15 years, and seven of them began after 2000. However, the intensity of the confl icts in Africa is higher than in other regions, which is probably linked to the fact that **the continent is home to almost half of the highest intensity confl icts in the world: DR Congo (east),**

Somalia, Sudan (south) and Uganda (north). With regard to the evolution of the wars in Africa in 2009, we should note the increase in violence in southern Sudan (mainly due to communal fighting) and Somalia (where some analysts have denounced the greatest escalation in violence of the last two decades) or the expansion of the LRA armed group into the Central African Republic, Sudan and DR Congo. On a positive note, we should highlight the decrease of violence in conflicts such as those in Chad, Nigeria (Niger Delta) or Sudan (Darfur).

In Asia, contrary to what happens in Africa, over 70% of the armed conflicts are linked to demands for

self-government or identity issues and the majority (64%) is highly internal. However, there are also situations with a clear international dimension, such as the cases of Afghanistan, India (Jammu and Kashmir) and Pakistan (northeast). The average duration of the conflicts in Asia surpasses 26 years and is clearly the highest in the world. In this sense, it should be noted that two of the oldest insurgencies on the planet (the Karen in Myanmar and the Naga in northeast India) can trace their origins back to the 1950s, while the two main communist insurgencies on the continent (the NPA in Philippines and the CPI-M in India) began their activities in the 1960s. In addition, there are five other conflicts
– Philippines (Mindanao-MILF), India (Assam),

India (Manipur), India (Jammu and Kashmir) or Sri Lanka (northeast)– that have been active for over two decades.

Some of the factors that may explain the long duration of the armed conflicts in Asia is the limited presence of international actors in facilitation and mediation tasks (especially by the United Nations), the large number of conflicts linked to the foundation of the State or the difficulty in resolving disputes linked to identity and selfdetermination, which are frequent in Asia. As far as intensity is concerned, we should point out that three of the nine conflicts that have the highest mortality rates on the planet are taking place in Southern Asia: Afghanistan, Pakistan (northeast) and Sri Lanka, in spite of the fact that this conflict ended in May. In regard to the actors, there is a mixture of conflicts on the Asian continent with some armed groups having significant war capability and control of territory –the CPIM in India, the NPA and the MILF in Philippines or the LTTE in Sri Lanka before their defeat in the first months of 2009– and other conflicts which are characterized by the fragmentation of the insurgent groups – Afghanistan, Pakistan (northeast), India (Assam), India (Nagaland), Myanmar or Thailand (south). Beyond the fact that practically all Governments use the term terrorist when referring to their respective armed opposition groups, of note are some cases such as Afghanistan,

Pakistan (northeast), India (Jammu and Kashmir) or Philippines (Mindanao-Abu Sayyaf) where the Governments have closely tied their counterinsurgency strategies to the socalled global war on terrorism which provides them with political legitimacy and in some cases with economic and military support. In the last cases listed the armed groups have made religious demands linked to Islam.

Another characteristic of the disputes in Asia is that there are some States, such as India, the Philippines or Pakistan, that are home to several armed conflicts, with different causes, war dynamics and locations. On the topic of the evolution of the conflicts in 2009, of note is the escalation of violence in Afghanistan and in northeast Pakistan —both with a growing involvement by the US Government– and the increase in counterinsurgency offensives by the Myanmar Government in the east of the country and the Philippine Government in Mindanao against the Abu Sayyaf group. Furthermore, it should also be noted the decline in hostilities in the Indian states of Jammu and Kashmir and Manipur. In another region in India, Nagaland, a signifi cant decrease in the number of deaths led this report to consider this the end of the armed confl ict. Also, the military victory by the Sri Lankan Armed Forces over the LTTE led to a drastic reduction in clashes and, thus, northeast Sri Lanka was no longer considered an armed conflict. However, in the final stages of the Army offensive, some of the most violent episodes of the war took place since its beginning in the 1980s.

Finally, there are some issues to consider with respect to the armed conflicts in the rest of the continents. In **America**, the conflict in Colombia continued to be one of the longest lasting and most lethal in the world, with a huge impact on the civilian population in terms of deaths and forced displacement. During 2009 violence increased in the southwestern regions of the country and the impact of the violence on the indigenous peoples was clear. In addition, the degree of internationalization of the conflict grew. In **Europe, the centre of disputes was again the area between the Black and Caspian seas**. In this region armed hostilities rose in the neighbouring Russian republics of Chechnya and Ingushetia due to the porous borders and a certain link between the insurgencies and the counterinsurgency policies. Nevertheless, in relative terms, the intensity of the conflict in both scenarios continued to be low. In Turkey, the different initiatives by the parties to resolve the conflict caused a decrease in the levels of violence, although armed clashes continued to be reported throughout the year and the Army continued to conduct bombing raids on the PKK in northern Iraq, where the group has its bases. Finally, in the **Middle East**, violence mounted in Iraq –mainly because of the proximity of the 2010 elections and the withdrawal of US troops from Iraqi cities– and especially in Yemen, where there is a risk of internationalization of the conflict due to the involvement of Saudi Arabia and Iran and greater attention by the West to al-Qaeda's activities in the country. Furthermore, the intensity of the conflict between Israel and Palestine diminished, especially because of the end to the Israeli military offensive in Gaza in the month of January. In the cases of Israel- Palestine and Yemen, the intensity of the conflict was medium, while the conflict in

Iraq continued to be one of the most virulent on the planet.

b) International missions

One of the questions in terms of global confl ict during 2009 that deserves mention is related to international missions. In December 2009 around the world there were 15 UN peacekeeping operations, two political missions run and supported by the UN Department of Peacekeeping Operations (BINUB and UNAMA) and another 10 UN political and peacekeeping operations supported by the UN Department of Political Affairs. From a regional perspective, of the 27 UN missions in the world, approximately half (13) were in the African conArmed Conflicts **25** (led by the United States 5th Fleet), together with other

ships, was launched to patrol Somali territorial waters
and the Gulf of Aden in the northwest Indian Ocean to
stop attacks on ships that fi sh or pass through the
area.
The UN peacekeeping missions were made up of around
120,000 troops7 and 3,781 more were on political and
peacebuilding missions which are above the numbers
for 2008. This clearly shows the continuous increase of
missions and forces that has taken place in the last
decade. Since June 1999, when the number reached
its lowest point since the end of the Cold War (13,000
Blue Helmets), to the present day, growth has been
constant and need are still dire in many

contexts. To this number we should also add the NATO forces (more than 83,000 troops), from the EU (over 6,000 troops including police and soldiers in six contexts, although the end of EUFOR TCHAD/RCA reduces this number to less than half), from the CIS (more than 4,200 troops tinent, five in the Middle East, five in Asia, three in Europe and one in America. In addition, alongside the United Nations, many other regional organizations participate in military, political and peacebuilding tasks such as the OSCE (with 19 missions in the European and Central Asian sphere), the EU (15 missions in Africa, Asia, Europe and the Middle East) and NATO (six missions in Europe, Asia, Africa and the Middle

East), the CIS (three missions in Europe), the AU (two missions in Africa), the OAS (two missions in America), the ECCAS (one mission in Africa) and seven multilateral operations under the auspices of countries or groups of countries. Changes that took place this year included not renewing the UN peacekeeping mission in Georgia, UNOMIG, as well as the two missions by the CIS in the Georgian regions of Abkhazia and South Ossetia. The EU mission EUFOR TCHAD/RCA successfully transferred its functions to the MINURCAT in March. Additionally, a joint sea operation by NATO (Operation Ocean Shield), the EU NAVFOR and Combined Task

Force 151

Table 1.2. **Main international missions in 2009**

Name	Start-End	Name	Start-End
UN		**NATO**	
West Africa (UNOWA)	2001	Afghanistan (ISAF)	2001
Burundi (BINUB)	2007	Iraq (NTIM-I)	2004
DR Congo (MONUC)	1999	Kosovo (KFOR)	1999
Côte d'Ivoire (ONUCI)	2004	Operation Active Endeavour (Mediterranean Sea)	2001
Guinea-Bissau (UNOGBIS)	2000	Horn of Africa, Gulf of Aden (Operation Ocean Shield)	2009
Liberia (UNMIL)	2003	**EU**	
Western Sahara (MINURSO)	1991	DR Congo (EUSEC DR Congo)	2005
Central African Rep. (BONUCA)	2000	Central African Rep. and Chad (EUFOR TCHAD/RCA)	2007-2009
Central African Rep. / Chad (MINURCAT)	2007	Palestine Territories (EU BAM Rafah)	2005
Sierra Leone (UNIPSIL)	2008	Palestine Territories (EUPOL COPPS)	2006
Somalia (UNPOS)	1995	Afghanistan (EUPOL Afghanistan)	2002

Sudan (UNMIS) 2005 Bosnia and Herzegovina (EUPM) 2003
Sudan (Darfur) (UNAMID) 2007 Bosnia and Herzegovina (EUFOR ALTHEA) 2004
Haiti (MINUSTAH) 2004 **CIS**
Afghanistan (UNAMA) 2002 Georgia (South Ossetia) 1992-2009
India and Pakistan (UNMOGIP) 1949 Georgia (Abkhazia) 1994-2009
Nepal (UNMIN) 2007 Moldova (Transdniestria) 1992
Timor-Leste (UNMIT) 2006 **ECCAS**
Central Asia (UNRCCA) 2007 Central African Rep. (MICOPAX) 2008
Cyprus (UNFICYP) 1964 **AU**
Georgia (Abkhazia) (UNOMIG) 1993-2009 Somalia (AMISOM) 2007
Kosovo (UNMIK) 1999 Comoros (MAES) 2007
Iraq (UNAMI) 2003 **Other missions**
Golan Heights (UNDOF) 1974 DPR Korea and Rep. of Korea (NSC) 1953
Lebanon (UNIFIL) 1978/2006 Solomon Islands (RAMSI) 2003
Lebanon (USCOL) 2007 Hebron, Palestine (TPIH

2) 1997
Middle East (UNTSO) 1948 Egypt and Israel 1982
Iraq (US and UK) 2003
Côte d'Ivoire (Operation Licorne, France) 2003
Timor-Leste (ISF, Australia) 2006

26 Alert 2010

in three contexts, although the two missions in Georgia
have concluded), ECCAS and the AU (almost 4,000
troops in three contexts), and another six operations
from different countries (close to 6,000 police offi cers
and soldiers). In general terms the total number of
peacekeeping troops deployed across the world easily
surpassed 210,000 soldiers and police offi cers. Moreover, if troops planned for in the design of the missions
or their extensions were actually deployed (nearly

7,000 Blue Helmets in the UNAMID in Darfur, close to
2,000 in the MONUC, 5,000 in the AMISOM are still
pending) the total would be 14,000 troops more. To
this number it could also be added 7,000 soldiers proposed
by the European countries and another 30,000
from the US for the ISAF in Afghanistan that will be
deployed between the end of 2009 and the beginning
of 2010. This would raise the number to over **260,000
soldiers deployed across the world in international missions.**
Finally, it must be added the joint sea operation
in the Indian Ocean made up of the EU NAVFOR, NATO
and the CTF 151 plus ships from other States such as
Japan, China, India and Saudi Arabia, although the

military figures for this operation are unknown. The growing use of Chapter VII of the United Nations Charter to design the mandate of the United Nations missions has led to a greater participation in violent scenarios. These multidimensional missions are being established in situations that are more and more violent and with mandates that are more and more complex, as can be seen by the number of deaths among UN troops, which have tripled since the end of the Cold War, rising from 800 in 1991 to 2,659 in December 2009. At the same time, the number of military operations designed using Chapter VII as a framework have increased in recent years with the consent of the UN

Security Council. An example of this is NATO/ISAF in Afghanistan, which is called a "coalition of goodwill". This is not a United Nations force *per se*, although it does have a mandate under the provisions of Chapter VII of the United Nations Charter and is conducting offensive operations independently, with US troops and to support the Afghan Government.

c) Arms embargoes

Furthermore, under the auspices of Chapter VII of the United Nations Charter, the Security Council may adopt coercive measures to maintain or re-establish international peace and security. These include economic or other kinds of sanctions, without the use of military force, or even international military intervention.8 The use of mandatory sanctions is intended to apply pressure on a State or entity to comply with the objectives set by the Security Council without resorting to the use of force.9 The sanctions can be economic or commercial in a broad sense, or more selective measures can be used such as arms embargoes, travel restrictions, financial or diplomatic restrictions, or both selective and general measures can be applied at the same time.

The EU also imposes binding arms embargoes for its Member States. In some cases they respond to the need to implement arms embargoes that the United Nations imposes and in other cases they are initiatives of the EU itself.

In 2009, 28 arms embargoes were in force for a total of 17 States and non-state armed groups. Of these, 12 embargoes were imposed by the United Nations and 16 by the EU.10 The UN Security Council passed resolution 1907 on December 23 which established a new arms embargo on Eritrea for violating the existing embargo on Somalia by providing political, financial and logistical aid, as well as training and arms to Somali Islamic armed groups opposed to the Somali Transitional Federal Government (TFG). The EU, in turn, imposed a new embargo on Guinea on October 27, due to the evolution of the situation in the country over the last year (10 days previously, ECOWAS had decided to impose a voluntary arms embargo for the Member States of the organization). The EU lifted the embargo on Uzbekistan on October 31 having considered that the human rights situation had improved in the country since the Andijan events, in spite of alerts from international organizations that there was a lack of any real advances. It is worth mentioning that 11 of the 16 embargoes established by the EU were to implement the UN Security Council embargoes.11 The remaining five correspond to initiatives by the EU: China, Myanmar, Guinea, Uzbekistan and Zimbabwe.

Of the 17 States and non-state armed groups indicated

by both organizations, six refer to currently active armed
confl icts (Myanmar, Sudan [Darfur] and armed groups in
Iraq, Somalia, DR Congo and Afghanistan). Of the other
11, eight refer to scenarios of socio-political crises of
varying intensity (China, Eritrea, Iran, Guinea, Lebanon,
DPR Korea, Uzbekistan and Zimbabwe) and the remaining
three have recently overcome armed confl icts and are
in post-war peacebuilding stages (Côte d'Ivoire, Liberia
and Sierra Leone) with different degrees of internal tension.
Beyond the criticism which can be levelled at embargoes
and their effectiveness, there are another 24
7. Of the 120,000 troops in UN peacekeeping missions, 98,114 are military and police personnel. 3% of this number (3,027 soldiers

and police officers) are women. Data available on December 8, 2009.

8. For more information on the UN Security Council Sanctions Committees please see <http://www.un.org/sc/committees/>.

9. The sanction mechanisms, and specifically arms embargoes, have been used inconsistently since the founding of the United Nations. Between 1945 and 1989 they were only used in two contexts tied to the decolonization process: in the former Southern Rhodesia (currently Zimbabwe) between 1968 and 1979 (due to internal instability); and in South Africa between 1977 and 1994 (because of South African intervention in neighbouring countries, internal violence and instability, and the system of racial discrimination or Apartheid). Forsaking the use of these mechanisms during the Cold War, as with other United Nations instruments, was part of the

politics of competition between the two Blocs, and
the end to the Cold War resulted in a growing activism by the organization in this area, and others, and paved the way to the imposition of arms
embargoes. Its use also strengthened the role of the United Nations as a cornerstone of international peace and security. In addition, arms
embargoes came to be seen as a more effective sanction than economic sanctions since they focused on the State elite and the non-state armed
groups, thus limiting their humanitarian impact.

10. There are two voluntary arms embargoes, one imposed by the OSCE on Armenia and Azerbaijan in 1992, and another imposed by ECOWAS on
Guinea in 2009.

11. In the case of Sudan, the EU imposed it for the entire country in 1994 and the UN Security Council for the Darfur region in 2004; in the case

of Iran they include different types of arms.
Armed Conflicts **27**
armed confl icts where neither the UN Security Council
nor the EU have proposed the establishment of an arms
embargo as a form of sanction. Furthermore, there are
another 60 situations of socio-political crisis of varying
intensity that have not been subject to embargoes and,
in many of these cases, the preventive nature of arms
embargoes could mean a decrease in the hostilities.

d) Military expenditure and armed conflict
Finally, an analysis of military expenditure as a percentage
of GDP of the countries in armed confl ict can help
us draw some conclusions. It should be noted that this
study is hampered by a lack of offi cial data,

which is frequent for many of the activities in the military sphere. Due to the situation in some of these countries, data are nonexistent, lower than actual fi gures and/or has been manipulated, since part of the expenditures related to State security activities are included in other areas of the budget. However, in most of the cases the percentage of government military expenditure as a percentage of GDP does not surpass 3%, with the exception of Algeria, Colombia, Pakistan, Russia, Israel and Yemen, six of the 20 countries with available data (no data exist for Somalia, Sudan and Palestine). Furthermore, according to SIPRI, it is estimated that worldwide military expenditure in 2007 reached 1339 billion USD which represents 25% of GDP in 2007.[12]

Thus, the first conclusion is that only in nine of the 20 countries in armed conflict military expenditure in 2007 was equal or above the anticipated world average for the year (India, Sri Lanka and Iraq are included with the six countries mentioned previously). In the other 11 cases military expenditure was lower than the world average.

However, this initial conclusion must be qualified by other factors. A factor that is not usually considered, but would necessarily increase the war machine figures in each context, is the resources managed by the political-military movements and their military wings.13

Only some approximate figures are available. The same may be said for international organizations or other countries that can be considered actors that are directly involved in the armed conflict due to their participation in the hostilities. In the case of armed groups, these figures can be a few thousand dollars a year, as in the case of some of the Mai Mai militias in DR Congo, or budgets of political-military movements whose organizational structure is much more complex. Examples of this last case include the FDLR in DR Congo, which

12. The estimated figure for 2008 is 1464 billion USD, which represents 2.4% of GDP in 2008. This figure is a 4% increase in real terms

compared to 2007 and a 45% rise since 1999. See SIPRI. *SIPRI Yearbook 2009. Armaments, Disarmament and International Security*. Oxford: Oxford University Press, 2009.

13. It must be noted that the total budget of armed groups is not dedicated to the war effort. They also include sections that are dedicated to maintaining their support networks and social policies, that is, resources that are not related to military aspects.

Table 1.3. **Arms embargoes currently in force declared by the United Nations, the EU and the OSCE**

Embargoes declared by the United Nations		**Embargoes declared by the EU**	
Country*	**Effective date**	**Country**	**Effective date**
Taliban militias and al-Qaeda**	2002	**Taliban militias and al-Qaeda***	2002
Côte d'Ivoire	2004	China	1989
Congo, DR (except the Government)	2003	Côte d'Ivoire	2004
Eritrea	2009	**Congo, DR (except the**	

Government) 2003
Iran 2006 Iran 2007
Iraq (except the Government) 2003 **Iraq (except the Government)** 2003
Lebanon (except the Government) 2006 Guinea 2009
Liberia (except the Government) 1992 Lebanon (except the Government) 2006
DPR Korea 2006 Liberia (except the Government) 2001
Sierra Leone (RUF) 1997 **Myanmar** 1991
Somalia (except the Government) 1992 DPR Korea 2006
Sudan (Darfur) (except the Government) 2004 Sierra Leone (RUF) 1998
Embargoes declared by the OSCE Somalia (except the Government) 2002
Armenia - Azerbaijan (Nagorno-Karabakh) 1992 **Sudan** 1994
Embargoes declared by ECOWAS Uzbekistan 2005-2009
Guinea 2009 Zimbabwe 2002

* In bold, country or group in armed conflict.
** Embargo that is not linked to a specific

country or territory.
Source: SIPRI. Arms Embargoes Database. 2009.
does not correspond to the military component of the
mission. In the case of UNAMID, this figure reached
1.598 billion dollars for the same period, making the
UNAMID the largest and most costly mission at present.
Although the UNAMID had not entered combat with the
different armed groups in Darfur or with the pro-government
militias, its mandate to protect the civilian population
may place the mission in a situation where they
must use force to avoid human rights violations. In the
case of NATO in Afghanistan, the ISAF's mandate is
backed by Chapter VII of the United Nations Charter, and
its main function is to aid the Afghan

Government to guarantee security in the country. Nevertheless, to implement that mandate it takes part in direct combat actions against different Taliban militias and other armed actors in the country and is therefore directly involved in the conflict. In this regard, the US budget for Afghanistan and in other countries (as part of Operation Enduring Freedom) has amounted to 159.8 billion dollars for the 2001-2008 period, with 34 billion corresponding to 2008. Finally, in the case of Iraq, the US budget was 603 billion dollars for the 2001-2008 period (153 billion for 2008, the highest figure since the operation was launched in 2003).[21]

1.3. Armed conflicts: annual evolution by region

Africa

a) Western Africa

Nigeria (Niger Delta)

Start: 2001

Type: Resources, Identity
Internal

Main parties: Government, MEND, MOSOP, NDPVF
and NDV, militias from the Ijaw, Itsekeri, Urhobo and Ogoni communities, private security groups

Intensity: 2

Trend: ?

Summary:
The conflict in the Niger Delta is the result of unsatisfied
demands for control of the profits from oil resources located in
that region. Several armed groups, MEND (Ijaw) is the most
noteworthy, demand compensation for the impact the extraction

industries have on their territory and a more equitable
share of the profits obtained from the installations and a greater
decentralization of the Nigerian State. Attacks on oil instal-

manages several millions of US dollars per year;15
Hamas, with an approximate budget of between 30 and
90 million dollars per year; Hezbollah, with a budget of
between 100 and 200 million dollars per year,16 or the
recently dismantled LTTE, with estimates of between
200 and 300 million dollars per year.17
There are also Governments and international organizations
that use military force, normally to support the
Governments of the countries affected by armed confl ict,
as part of a peace agreement or to verify

compliance with the ceasefire agreement. This intervention may be unilateral with no legal basis, or under a United Nations mandate, which gives it a legal basis and international legitimacy. Nevertheless, in some cases the coverage afforded by Chapter VII of the United Nations Charter, which allows the use of force,[18] converts the members of the international operations in parties of the armed conflict itself, although they have the legitimacy granted by the United Nations. An example of this are the two United Nations missions that are currently the most expensive and with the largest military component, the MONUC in the DR Congo, and the UNAMID[19] in the

Sudanese region of Darfur. In the case of the MONUC, which has participated in combat operations on several occasions on its own or to support the Congolese Armed Forces, its annual budget, 1.35 billion dollars,[20] is 10 times the amount of resources the Congolese Government dedicates to the war effort, although the entire 1.35 billion

14. In millions of US dollars. The percentage refers to the 2007 budget.
15. United Nations Security Council. *Final report of the Group of Experts on the DR Congo*. Letter dated 23 November 2009 addressed to the President of the Security Council from the Chairman of the Security Council Committee established pursuant to resolution 1533 (2004) concerning the DR Congo. November 23, 2009, in <http://www.un.org/Docs/sc/sgrep09.htm>.

16. Wallace, Bret. "Banks Are Not Mere Bystanders". The Terror Finance Blog, July 1, 2009, [consulted on 21.12.09], in <http://www.terrorfi-nance.org/Banks%20Are%20Not%20Mere%20Bystanders_Wallace.pdf>.

17. According to reports from Jane's Intelligence research centre cited in the Sri Lanka News, this figure is an estimation of the LTTE yearly budget. Jane's Intelligence stated that of that figure only nine million USD were needed for running their military activities. Sri Lanka News. "What if LTTE were Hamas & the GOSL were Israel with powerful friends?". January 10, 2009, in <http://www.lankanewspapers.com/news/2009/1/37519_space.html>.

18. Article 42 of the Charter states that the UN Security Council may take such action as necessary to maintain or restore international peace and security.

19. African Union/United Nations Hybrid

operation in Darfur.
20. For the approved period between July 1, 2009 and June 30, 2010.
21. SIPRI, 2009, op. cit.

Table 1.4. **Military expenditure in countries that are the scene of armed conflict, 2007** [14]

Country	Military expenditure (percentage of GDP)	Country	Military expenditure (percentage of GDP)
Algeria	3,515 (3%)	India	23,535 (2.5%)
Chad	64.2 (0.96%)	Myanmar	--
Ethiopia	285 (1.7%)	Pakistan	4,468 (3.1%)
Nigeria	816 (0.6%)	Sri Lanka	795 (2.8%)
Central African Rep.	16.1 (1.1%)	Thailand	2,569 (1.3%)
DR Congo	169 (2%)	Russia	34,800 (3.5%)

Somalia -- Turkey 11,155 (2.1%)
Sudan -- Iraq 828 (2.5%)
Uganda 237 (2.2%) Israel 12,513 (8.6%)
Colombia 5,579 (4%) Palestine --
Afghanistan 178 (2.2%) Yemen 821 (5.1%)
Philippines 1,034 (0.9%)
Source: SIPRI. *SIPRI Yearbook* 2009.

lations and military posts, as well as kidnappings of workers,
are the methods normally used by the insurgency. In addition,
this situation has led to fighting for control of the land and
resources by the different communities that live in the region.
During the year important advances took place which
could have led to the resolution of the conflict in the
Delta.22 However, at the beginning of 2009 the outlook
was not especially good since the MEND called off the

ceasefire that had been declared in September 2008
and they threatened to launch a large scale offensive.
Dozens of deaths and kidnappings occurred at the beginning
of the year. The gas and oil supply was interrupted
and there were attacks on oil platforms and Police stations.
The situation got worse on May 15 with the offensive
mounted by the governmental military unit **Joint
Task Force (JTF)**. The JTF is responsible for security in
the Delta. This offensive was the most serious in recent
years, lasted three weeks and caused **hundreds of deaths
and the displacement of thousands of people**. This provoked
a response by the MEND with new kidnappings and attacks on the oil industry. After this

operation, on June 25 the president declared **a ceasefire, an amnesty for members of the groups that abandoned armed combat in 60 days time and he freed one of the MEND leaders, Henry Okah.** As a result, **the MEND announced a temporary ceasefire** –for 60 days starting July 15– to facilitate the beginning of talks. This ceasefire was later extended for a month and then, in October, was made indefinite. Nevertheless, divisions in the MEND regarding the acceptance of the amnesty, and the existence of sectors that did not obey the orders from the leaders to demobilize, threatened to jeopardize the process. Moreover, mistrust by the MEND continued and on several occasions they threatened to renew fighting if advances were not achieved in the negotiation process, and due to some sporadic episodes with the JTF, and delays in the beginning

of the rehabilitation program. At the end of the year
15,000 insurgents were included in the disarmament
process, according to the Government.

b) Horn of Africa

Ethiopia (Ogaden)

Start: 2007
Type: Self-government, Identity
Internal
Main parties: Government, ONLF, OLF, progovernment
militias
Intensity: 2
Trend: =
Summary:
Ethiopia has experienced secessionist movements or resistance
to central power since the 1970s. The ONLF was founded
in 1984 and operates in the Ethiopian region of Ogaden, in
the southeast of the country, and demands a greater degree of

autonomy for the Somali community that lives in the region.
On several occasions the ONLF has conducted insurgent activities
beyond the Ogaden region in collaboration with the OLF
which demands from the Government greater autonomy for
the region of Oromia since 1973. The Somali Government has
backed the ONLF against Ethiopia, who it went to war with for
control of the region in 1977 and 1978. In this war Ethiopia
defeated Somalia. The end to the war between Eritrea and
Ethiopia in 2000 led to an increase in government operations
to bring to an end the insurgency in Ogaden, and after the
2005 elections, fighting between the Armed Forces and the
ONLF have been on the rise.
During the year there were **attacks and**

ambushes by the ONLF on the security forces and its garrisons, as well as military operations by the Army and the pro-government militias, although this information could not be confirmed due to the restrictive information policy of the Government and limited access to the Ethiopian region of Ogaden. Even United Nations requests to access to the area were rejected. In mid-November, the ONLF announced the death of 626 Ethiopian soldiers and that it had captured seven towns, and military material and vehicles in different attacks conducted by the groups in the areas near the Somali border. The Government, which had previously announced in October that the ONLF was no longer a security threat, again denied the claims. According to the Government, the army offensive conducted in 2007 had dismantled the military capability of the ONLF. Simultaneously, the Malay multinational company Petronas, together with other foreign companies participating in the extraction of hydrocarbons in the region, was warned by the ONLF on several occasions of the consequences of collaborating with the Government since it is considered an accomplice of the serious situation of violence that troubles the area. Meanwhile, the Government continued in its attempt to convince this company and others that the ONLF no longer had the capability to attack oil exploration and production in the region. There was an upsurge of local denouncements of abuses and attacks by the Army and its militias against the civilian population, and Addis Ababa confirmed the execution of one of the ONLF leaders, Serad Dolal. The Internal Displacement Monitoring Centre estimated that 300,000 people continued to be displaced during 2009 as a consequence of the different inter-community conflicts and border disputes that affected the country.

Somalia

Start: 1988
Type: Government
Internationalized internal
Main parties: New Transitional Federal Government (TFG) —which was joined by the moderate faction of the Alliance for the Reliberation of Somalia (ARS), and supported by Ahl as-Sunna wal-Jama'a, warlords, Ethiopia, US, AMISOM-, Alliance for the Reliberation of Somalia radical faction (ARS) —which includes partly the Union of Islamic Courts (UIC), Hizbul Islam, al-Shabab- and is supported by Eritrea

22. See Chapter 3 (Peace processes).

The United Nations

denounced that all of the parties in the conflict were committing acts of torture and deliberate attacks on civilians, which could be classified as war crimes

30 Alert 2010

Intensity: 3
Trend: =
Summary:
The armed conflict and the lack of effective central authority in the country began in 1988 when a coalition of opposition groups rebelled against the dictatorial power of Siad Barre, and three years later they were able to depose him. This led to a new fight within the coalition to fill the vacuum of power which has caused the destruction of the country

and the death of 300,000 people since 1991, in spite of the failed international intervention at the beginning of the 1990s. Various peace processes set up to create a central authority have run into numerous difficulties, including grievances between different clans and subclans which make up the Somali social structure, interference by Ethiopia and Eritrea, and the power of different warlords. The most recent peace initiative created in 2004 the TFG, which has been backed by Ethiopia in an attempt to regain control of the country which is partially in the hands of the UIC. The moderate faction of the UIC has joined the TFG and together they fight against the militias of the radical faction of the UIC which control part of the southern region of the country.

Despite the remodelling of the Transitional Federal Government in January which includes sectors linked to the ARS, among them Sheikh Sharif Sheikh Ahmed – the new president who replaces Abdullahi Yusuf Ahmed–, fighting continued throughout the year in different areas in the centre and south between the **TFG –backed by the moderate militia Ahl as-Sunna wal-Jama'a and by the AMISOM– against the insurgency made up of al-Shabab and Hizbul Islam.** In September **fighting between al-Shabab and allied factions of Hizbul Islam** took place for several reasons, among which was the control and management of the lucrative port of

Kismayo, in the south, and the fact that some representative figures from Hizbul Islam joined the TFG. The presence of Ethiopian Armed Forces in Somalia was reported at different times during the year to give support to the TFG and pursue the insurgency. This was denied by Ethiopia. The US also carried out unilateral actions –bombardments– as part of the persecution of alleged members of al-Qaeda in the country that would have links to al-Shabab. At the beginning of Ramadan, the worst escalation of violence in the past 20 years broke out according to the local Elman Peace and Human Rights Organisation. Several sources have reported that **17,000 people have died since the beginning**

of 2007. Al-Shabab threatened to extend the war to the Horn of Africa region. According to the TFG, thousands of foreigners entered the country to join al-Shabab with the goal of overthrowing it. The United Nations High Commissioner for Human Rights denounced that all of the parties in the confl ict were committing acts of torture and deliberate attacks on civilians, which could be classifi ed as war crimes. The United Nations warned that the country was going through its worst humanitarian crisis since 1991.23 The TFG, unable to deal with the internal situation and piracy,24 requested the strengthening of the AMISOM o its substitution by a more robust United Nations mission.

Sudan (Darfur)

Start: 2003
Type: Self-government, Resources, Identity
Internationalized internal
Main parties: Government, pro-government Janjaweed
militias, JEM, several factions of the
SLA and other armed groups
Intensity: 2
Trend: ?
Summary:
The conflict in Darfur began in 2003 related to demands of
greater decentralisation and development of the region by several
insurgent groups, mainly the SLA and the JEM. The Government
responded to this uprising by using its own Armed
Forces and the Arab Janjaweed militias. The magnitude of the
violence committed by all contending parties against the civilian

population has led some to consider the possibility that genocide has taken place in the region. 300,000 people have died since the beginning of hostilities according to the United Nations. After a peace agreement (DPA) was signed between the government and one faction of the SLA in May 2006, levels of violence grew and brought about the fragmentation of the opposition groups and a serious regional impact due to the displacement of the population caused by the Sudanese implication in the Chadian conflict and the Chadian implication in the Sudanese conflict. An observation mission by the AU (AMIS), created in 2004, was included in 2007 in a joint UN and AU mission, the UNAMID. This mission has been attacked multiple

times. In 2008 it did not reach even half of the planned 26,000
troops and therefore is unable to comply with its mission to
protect the civilian population and humanitarian personnel.

The situation in Darfur was marked by the **arrest order,
announced in March, by the International Criminal
Court (ICC) against the Sudanese president accused of
war crimes and crimes against humanity** in the region.

The Government reacted by expelling the international
humanitarian organizations from the country which gave
rise to international condemnation and concern that the
humanitarian situation would deteriorate. It also generated
an important controversy between those in favour

and those against the ICC decision. Afterwards, the order to expel the NGOs was partially revoked. During the year, the United Nations was able to see a gradual decline of fighting, although it underlined the volatility of the situation.25 Even the general of the UNAMID Martin Agwai stated that the war had ended. His statement was strongly criticized. The Panel of Experts on

23. See Chapter 5 (Humanitarian crises).
24. Given the persistence of piracy in the waters of the Gulf of Aden, with more than 140 attacks and fifty kidnappings of ships that were navigating within and outside the security zone patrolled by the international community, the special representative of UN secretary-general Somalia noted that the fight against piracy cannot be limited to the deployment of international naval forces,

and added that the only sustainable solution is the establishment of an effective government and security institutions and provide alternative sources of income to the population. The lack of a central Government in the country, the general atmosphere of impunity and the very high economic benefits that kidnappings provide facilitate
that several militias in the region of Puntland are increasingly getting involved in this activity, given the regional authorities' inability to control
the situation, when they are not involved.
25. UN Security Council. *Report of the Secretary-General on the deployment of the African Union-United Nations Hybrid Operation in Darfur.*
S/2009/352, 13 July 2009, in <http://www.un.org/Docs/journal/asp/ws.asp?m=S/2009/352>.
Armed Conflicts **31**
the arms embargo stated in November that actions of
war had continued.26 They denounced the

systematic failure to comply with the embargo by all of the parties involved in the conflict, violations of human rights and abuses of the civilian population, especially against women, as well as the disproportionate use of force by the Sudanese Army and paramilitary groups. Finally, the Panel evaluated the violation of the embargo in the context of four issues that continued to affect Darfur: competition for land and resources; the rape of women and impunity in Darfur; the war between the armed groups and the Governments of Sudan and Chad, with the Sudanese JEM and Chadian groups being the main actors; and finally, the cross-border attacks carried out by the Sudanese and Chadian Armies. Moreover, over two years after its creation, the UNAMID did not complete its deployment and suffered an increase in the

number
of attacks. 2.6 million people continued to be displaced
and another 4.7 million relied on humanitarian aid.27

Sudan (South)

Start: 2009
Type: Territory, Resources, Self-government
Internal
Main parties: Militias of ethnic groups, National Unity
Government, the semi-autonomous
Government of South Sudan, political
parties of the south
Intensity: 3
Trend: ?
Summary:
After signing in 2005 the peace agreement between the SPLA
armed group from the south and the Government of Sudan,
which ended an armed conflict that set the north against the
south for 20 years, inter-communal rivalry in

the south reappeared at the scene of violence. The communities, which were fighting for control of resources and pastureland, initially limited their actions to stealing each others livestock. Since the end of 2008, however, there was a change in the pattern of violence with direct attacks on towns, deaths of members of the civilian population and kidnapping of children. The Government of South Sudan accused the NCP, the party of Sudan's president, of being behind the violence. Several analysts, however, suggested the possibility that different political groups from the south might also be interested in demonstrating the infeasibility of the political project of the SPLM, political wing of the former armed group,

in light of
the referendum planned for 2011 which will decide whether
the south splits away from the north.
**During the year there was a sharp rise in inter-communal
fi ghting, mainly in the state of Jonglei, but also in Lakes,
Unity and Central Equatoria**. Most of the clashes were
between militias of the Murle, Lou-Nuer, Dinka, Mundari
y Shilluk communities and **the number of deaths since
the beginning of 2009 has easily surpassed 2,500 victims**.
More than 350,000 people have abandoned their
homes in southern Sudan due to the violence in the region.
Several analysts pointed to a change in the pattern
of inter-communal violence which had gone
from clashes between farmers to direct attacks

on villages and the kidnapping of children. The proximity of the general elections (February 2010) and the referendum (2011) —which will determine the possible secession of the south— could be behind the instability. In some cases the target seemed to be the SPLA security forces, which contradicted the government position which stated that the origin of the violence was competition for livestock. The analyses also mentioned internal factors as the cause for the disputes and the existence of local rivalries —even within the SPLA itself— regarding the elections.

The SPLA accused the Army and the NCP, president Omar al-Bashir's party, of providing arms and munitions to the militias of the southern states in an attempt to hinder the SPLA's efforts to disarm the civilian population. Khartoum, meanwhile, criticized the lack of action by the

Government of the south. In this sense, the United Nations described the situation in the south of the country as a security vacuum, where the different communities depended on their own militias of armed young men to defend themselves from attacks and livestock theft.

c) Great Lakes and Central Africa

DR Congo (East)
Start: 1998
Type: Government, Identity, Resources
Internationalized internal
Main parties: Government, Mai-Mai militias, FDLR, FDLR-RUD, CNDP, FRF, PARECO, APCLS, armed Ituri groups, Burundian FNL armed opposition group, Ugandan ADF-NALU and LRA armed opposition group, Rwanda, MONUC
Intensity: 3
Trend: =
Summary:

The current conflict originated with the coup d'état carried out
by Laurent Desiré Kabila in 1996 against Mobutu Sese Seko,
which eventually led him to relinquish power in 1997. In
1998, Burundi, Rwanda and Uganda, together with various
armed groups, attempted to overthrow Kabila, who in turn
received support from Angola, Chad, Namibia, Sudan and
Zimbabwe, in a war that has left around four million dead.
Control and exploitation of the country's natural resources
have contributed to the perpetuation of the conflict and the
presence of foreign Armed Forces. The signing of a ceasefire
agreement in 1999 and various peace agreements in 2002
and 2003 led to the withdrawal of foreign troops and the creation

of a transitional government and subsequently an elected
government in 2006. This has not meant an end to violence in
the east of the country, given Rwanda's involvement and the
presence of factions that have not yet been demobilised, as
well as the FDLR, which was responsible for the genocide in
Rwanda in 1994.

26. UN Security Council. *Report by The Panel of Experts established pursuant to resolution 1591 (2005) concerning Sudan.* S/2009/562, 29 October 2009, in <http://www.un.org/Docs/journal/asp/ws.asp?m=S/2009/562>.

27. See Chapter 4 (Humanitarian crises).

In southern Sudan
there was an
increase in intercommunal
violence
that easily surpassed
2,500 deaths since

the beginning of 2009

At the beginning of 2009, a series of events took place that shaped the rest of the year: tensions in the CNDP armed group resulted in an internal coup d'état. The military leader of the group, Bosco Ntaganda, replaced the leader Laurent Nkunda, and subsequently ended the hostilities against the Congolese Armed Forces (FARDC) and then integrated the armed group into them, with the consent of Rwanda. In an agreement on March 23, the CNDP certified its transformation into a political party in exchange for amnesty and the liberation of those under arrest. Nevertheless, the CNDP also maintained its structure and political control in North Kivu, in spite of the fact that it merged with the FARDC. Rwanda and DR Congo had been negotiating a rapprochement which resulted in the dismantling of this group. Additionally, in January and February the joint operation in Congolese territory between the Armed Forces from both countries against the Rwandese FDLR apparently resulted in a weakening of the armed group. However, at a later time the operation was considered a failure since **the FDLR regained the positions it had abandoned during the offensive, and a group of UN experts stated that the group's command structure was**

still intact in spite of the operation, and maintained the same illegal funding mechanisms. Several analysts also stated that **the DDR process for the 25 or more Mai Mai militias and the reform of the security sector had been a failure due to corruption and poor management of the resources.** In March the FARDC operation, Kimia II, was launched with logistic support from the MONUC in an attempt to neutralize the FDLR. Systematic violations of human rights and sexual violence were perpetrated,[28] which raised contradictions in the MONUC. In November, Germany arrested the FDLR leader, Ignace Murwanashyaka, and his vice commander, Straton

Musoni, who are accused of crimes of war and crimes
against humanity.
Central African Republic
Start: 2006
Type: Government
Internationalized internal
Main parties: Government, APRD, UFRD, armed groups split from UFDR (FURCA, MJLC), FDPC, CPJP, France, FOMUC, MINURCAT and Zaraguinas (highway bandits)
Intensity: 1
Trend: =
Summary:
In 2006, the situation in the country deteriorated considerably
as a result of increased activities by a number of insurgent
groups who dispute the legitimacy of the François Bozizé government,
which took power following a coup d'état against
President Ange Félix Patassé during 2002 and

2003. The Bozizé Government has been accused of mismanaging public funds and dividing the nation. The insurgency fights on two fronts: first, in the densely populated central and north-western parts of the country, the APRD, led by Jean-Jacques Demafouth, has challenged the Bozizé government and demanded a new sharing of power. Secondly, there has been an increase in insurgency operations in the northeast of the country by groups belonging to the UFDR coalition. To this instability was added the emergence in the north-west of numerous bands of highway bandits, the Zaraguinas. Instability persisted and the implementation of the peace agreements was slow. Nevertheless, at the beginning of the year the armed groups APRD and UFDR were included in the Government. In July, the leader of the FDPC armed group, Abdoulaye Miskine, signed a peace agreement that had been pending since 2008. **Several international organizations alerted to the gradual escalation of violence and insecurity due to actions by criminal groups, State security forces and armed groups which mainly affected the civilian population.** In October, Miskine torpedoed the peace process by stating that the Government had failed to implement the peace agreements of 2007 and 2009, and declared them invalid. Shortly after, his group, the FDPC, launched attacks against the Central African Army.

The CPJP, the only armed group that had not joined the
peace process to date, conducted various small military
operations throughout the year and demanded that negotiations
begin. At the end of the year, MINURCAT only had
2,750 of the planned 5,200 soldiers, 53% of the forces
needed to guarantee the fulfilment of its mandate. The
Government presented its DDR program in August. It is
anticipated that between 6,000 and 10,000 insurgents
will participate. Of note were some advances which took
place in the political sphere. In October, the **Government
enacted the election law, accepted by the opposition** that
had threatened to withdraw from the process, and **days**

later the election commission was set up. However, preparations
for the presidential elections in March 2010 were
delayed for numerous reasons. Former president Ange
Félix Patassé returned from exile at the end of October to
participate in the elections. Furthermore, the Ugandan
LRA armed group stepped up its activities in the southeast
of the country with kidnappings that forced the displacement
of over 4,500 people.29

Chad

Start: 2006
Type: Government
Internationalized internal
Main parties: Government, new UFR coalition of
armed groups (UFDD, UFDDFundamental, RFC, CNT, FSR, UFCD,
UDC, FPRN), MDJT, FPIR, Janjaweed

militias, Toro Boro militia, Sudan, France

Intensity: 2
Trend: ?
Summary:
The frustrated *coup d'état* of 2004 and the reform of the Constitution in 2005, boycotted by the opposition, sparked the insurgency that intensified its activity during 2006, with the aim of overthrowing the authoritarian government of Idriss Déby. This opposition is made up of several groups and soldiers hostile to the regime. In addition there is the antagonism that exists between Arab tribes and black populations in the border region between Sudan and Chad which is linked to

28. See Chapter 6 (Gender).
29. See Uganda (north).

local grievances, competition for resources and the extension of the war to the neighbouring Sudanese region of Darfur as a result of cross-border operations by Sudanese armed groups and Sudanese pro-government Arab *Janjaweed* militias. These groups have attacked towns and Darfur refugee camps in eastern Chad, which has contributed to an escalation of tension between Sudan and Chad, which accuse each other of supporting the other's respective insurgencies. Of note is the establishment between November 2008 and January 2009 of a new armed coalition, the Union of Resistance Forces (UFR), made up of eight armed groups including the main factions: the RFC of Timane Erdimi (chosen as leader of the coalition) and

Mahamat Nouri's UFDD. Previous coalitions had failed because of divisions and rivalries regarding issues of leadership. This coalition launched in May an important offensive from Sudan and the Chadian Army responded by pursuing the rebel groups in Sudanese territory. The fighting caused 250 deaths (the majority from the rebel forces) and hundreds of wounded, according to the Chadian Government. Chad's incursion in Sudanese territory unleashed a new diplomatic crisis between both countries.

30 Nevertheless, in July a new coalition of three groups, the National Movement, **signed a peace agreement with the Chadian Government in Sirte (Libya) with**

the intermediation of Muammar Gaddafi. It included a halt to hostilities, a general amnesty, and the possibility for the armed groups to participate in political activities and join the Armed Forces.31 The UFR coalition of Timane Erdimi rejected this agreement and called for the establishment of an inclusive negotiating table. At the end of the year, MINURCAT only had 2,750 of the planned 5,200 soldiers, 53% of the forces needed to guarantee the fulfilment of its mandate. As an example, almost 200 attacks on humanitarian personnel took place in 2009. In the political sphere, the Government and the opposition made advances in the implementation

of the agreement of August 2007 and agreed to create an election commission. However, the political
environment continued to be affected by the lack of a
solution to the confl ict, as pointed out by the UN
Secretary General.32

Uganda (North)

Start: 1986
Type: Self-government, Identity
Internationalized internal
Main parties: Ugandan Armed Forces, Central African,
Congolese and from South Sudan, pro-government militias from DR Congo
and from South Sudan, LRA
Intensity: 3
Trend: ?
Summary:
Since 1986, northern Uganda has been suffering from a conflict
in which the LRA armed opposition group, moved by the

religious messianism of its leader, Joseph Kony, has been trying
to overthrow the government of Yoweri Museveni, to establish
a regime based on the Ten Commandments of the Bible
and to bring the northern region of the country out of its marginalisation.
The violence and insecurity caused by the LRA's attacks against the civilian population, the kidnapping of children
to swell their ranks (around 25,000 since the beginning
of the conflict) and the confrontations between the armed
group and the Armed Forces (together with the pro-governmental
militias) have caused the death of around 200,000
people and the forced displacement of nearly two million people
at the height of the conflict. The LRA has expanded its
activities in neighbouring countries where it set

up bases, due to the inability in DR Congo and the Central African Republic to stop them, and with the complicity of Sudan. Between 2006 and 2008, a peace process had been ongoing and had managed to stop hostilities, although it failed and in December 2008, the Ugandan, Congolese and South Sudan (SPLA) Armies carried out an offensive against the LRA. This caused the group to split up and move to the north of DR Congo, the southeast of the Central African Republic and the south-west of Sudan where the offensive continued. **During the year a constant trickle of attacks by the LRA took place in the region made up of the provinces of Haut-Uélé and Bas Uélé (north and northeast of DR

Congo), Haut Mbomou (southeast of the Central African
Republic), and in towns of the neighbouring states in
southern Sudan, Western Equatoria and Western Bahr
al-Ghazal, near the Congolese and Central African border.
The humanitarian agencies that work in the region
denounced the death of 2,000 civilians since December
2008. Additionally, there were reports of plundering
and the kidnapping of hundreds of people. This highlighted
the fact that the LRA was made up of many small groups with certain freedom of action, according
to different analysts. The military operations to dismantle
the LRA had pushed the group (or some of its units,
mainly the one led by Joseph Kony, who was

allegedly in the Central African Republic) farther and farther to the north. This fragmented the group and its makeup became more international. Dozens of LRA members surrendered during the year reducing its numbers to several hundred combatants, the majority children, although the group did not lose its lethal capacity. Attacks by the LRA forced the displacement of 70,000 Sudanese, and some 5,000 Congolese sought refuge in the Sudanese state of Western Equatoria. Given the magnitude of the problem, the UN Security Council called for its peacekeeping missions in the Central African Republic (MINURCAT), DR Congo (MONUC) and southern Sudan (UNMIS) to coordinate its strategies to protect the civilian population from LRA attacks.

d) Maghreb and North Africa

Algeria

Start: 1992

Type: System
Internationalized internal

Main parties: Government, Salafist Group for Preaching and Combat (GSPC) /
al-Qaeda in the Islamic Maghreb (AQIM)

Intensity: 2

30. See Chapter 2 (Socio-political crises).
31. See Chapter 3 (Peace processes).
32. UN Security Council. *Report of the Secretary-General on the United Nations Mission in the Central African Republic and Chad.* S/2009/535, 14 October 2009, in <http://www.un.org/Docs/journal/asp/ws.asp?m=S/2009/535>.
34 Alert 2010

Trend: =

Summary:
This conflict began with the banning of the Islamic Salvation

Front (FIS) in 1992 after it had won the municipal (1990) and
legislative (1991) elections, defeating the party that had historically
led the country to independence, the National Liberation
Front. The victory of the FIS took place in the context of a
growing Islamic movement in the 1970s in response to popular
unrest which was further exacerbated in the 1980s by the
economic crisis and the lack of opportunity for political participation.
After the military chiefs of staff banned the FIS and
dismissed the government, a period of armed struggle began
between a number of groups (the EIS, the GIA and the GSPC,
which split off from the GIA and became AQIM in 2007) and
the army, backed by self-defence militias. The conflict left

150,000 dead during the 1990s, the majority of them civilians, amid accusations of army and Islamist groups' involvement in massacres. In spite of the reconciliation processes promoted by the government, the conflict is ongoing and has claimed thousands of lives since 2000. Episodes of violence continued in the context of the confl ict between the Government and al-Qaeda in the Islamic Maghreb (AQIM) and **caused more than 300 deaths in incidents throughout the country and in border regions** during 2009. The former Salafi st Group for Preaching and Combat (GSPC) celebrated its third year as a branch of al-Qaeda in the region and continued with attacks on the military, police and security guards, although it also caused civilian casualties. As part of its counterinsurgency campaign, the Government reported throughout the year the number of rebels captured and those who surrendered. In November AQIM leader, Abdelmalek Droukdel, was sentenced to death in absentia along with fifty of his followers for an attack in 2007 that caused 11 deaths in Algiers. Together with the military campaign, the Algerian Government also launched a media offensive to question the Islamic cause of AQIM. In this context, some former GSPC leaders made a public statement calling for AQIM to abandon violence and accept the amnesty offered by the Government. In the political sphere, it should be noted that **insurgent activity redoubled at the time of the controversial April elections in which president Abdelaziz Bouteflika was re-elected to a third term** with over 90% of the vote. In parallel to the armed offensive, AQIM continued with its campaign of kidnappings. Often the victims were people from the West captured in neighbouring countries such as Mali or Niger. In November and December alone AQIM captured three Spaniards and two Italians in Mauritania and a French national in Mali. **In response to the expansion of the group's actions into the Sahel region, during 2009 regional cooperation initiatives were set in**

motion to battle AQIM. This included forces from Algeria,
Mali, Niger and Mauritania.

Box 1.1. **Al-Qaeda in the Islamic Maghreb: Origins, tactics and new areas of action**

Efforts by several countries in North Africa to coordinate their anti-terrorism strategies in 2009 could be attributed to a growing concern regarding the actions of al-Qaeda in the Islamic Maghreb (AQIM) beyond the borders of Algeria, the country were
it arose in January 2007. Although this may seem recent, the truth is that this franchise of Osama bin Laden's network is the
continuation of the Salafist Group for Preaching and Combat (GSPC), which played an important role in the Islamic struggle
against the Algerian Government at the end of the 1990s. Despite the name change, the group's actions have always been
seen as part of a strictly domestic insurgency. Nevertheless, in recent years AQIM's operations have raised concern in the
region and in European countries which have

posed questions regarding their objectives, tactics and sphere of action.
In this context, one should analyze the origin of AQIM and its evolution after the Algerian GSPC. The latter had its roots in
the internecine struggle set off in the country at the beginning of the 1990s when the Military regime decided to cancel the
second round of elections when a victory by the Islamic movement seemed evident. The bloody internal war was witness to
the emergence of several groups in protest against the Government. Among them was the Armed Islamic Group (GIA) who was
accused of being responsible for multiple actions against the Algerian security forces and massacres and abuses of the civilian
population. In 1998, the GSPC was born when the group split off from the GIA allegedly due to differences regarding the
tactics used by the latter group that affected the civilian population. The members of the new GSPC considered these tactics counterproductive to achieve the goal of

building an Islamic State. The GSPC, which had some veteran Algerian Mujahideen members from the war in Afghanistan against the soviets (1979 – 1989), rejected an offer of peace from the Government –which other organizations did accept– as well as the Charter for Peace and National Reconciliation, and became the most active Islamic armed organization in Algeria. A key date for the GSPC was 2003, the year it chose a leadership in favour of maintaining the Jihad against the Algerian Government and open to joining the al-Qaeda cause. Factors such as the designation of the GSPC as a terrorist group by Washington after the attacks in 2001, religious motivations, the beginning of the war in Iraq – which boosted the recruitment of new members–, the decision to revitalize the movement and the possibility to extend its contacts with other militant groups, are some of the elements that would have favoured contacts with the network of Osama bin Laden, which was channelled through the al-Qaeda leader in Iraq, the late Abu Musab al-Zarqawi. Some investigations indicate that the ties were from much earlier on and that bin Laden himself had allocated funds for the creation of the GSPC at the end of the 1990s. Nevertheless, at least publically, it was not until September 11, 2006 when al-Qaeda admitted the tie to the GSPC. Four months later it was renamed AQIM.33 Even though the group's main objective is linked to overthrowing the Algerian regime and the creation of an Islamic caliphate –some analysts feel that this is the genuine agenda and doubt that AQIM is a regional organization

33. For more information, see Mekhennet, Souad. "Ragtag Insurgency Gains a Lifeline from al-Qaeda", *The New York Times*, July 1 2008, in <http://www.nytimes.com/2008/07/01/world/africa/01algeria.html#> and Hansen, Andrew. *Backgrounder: Al Qaeda in the Islamic Maghreb*. Washington DC: Council on Foreign Relations, July 21 2009,

in <http://www.cfr.org/publication/12717>.

34. See Joffe, George. "A convenient untruth", *The Guardian*, April 12 2007, in <http://www.guardian.co.uk/commentisfree/2007/apr/12/aconvenientuntruth>.

35. See Europol. *EU Terrorism Situation and Trend Report*. The Hague: Europol, 2009, in <http://www.europol.europa.eu/publications/EU_Terrorism_ Situation_and_Trend_Report_TE-SAT/TESAT2009.pdf>.

36. See Tawill, Camille. "New Strategies in al-Qaeda's Battle for Algeria". *Terrorism Monitor*, Volume VII, 22, (July 27 2009), in <http://www.jamestown.org/uploads/media/TM_007_63.pdf>.

37. See Chikhi, Lamine. " Algeria sponsors Sufism to Fight Extremism". *Reuters*, July 8 2009, in <http://in.reuters.com/article/oilRpt/idINL721135820090708>.

that acts coherently–,34 in public statements the group has broadened its objectives to include attacks on European and US interests, and asserts that it has expanded its activities and recruiting to neighbouring countries in the Maghreb and the Sahel.

In videos and communiqués on the web, AQIM leader, Abdelmalek Droukdel —an explosives expert who goes by the name of Abu Musab Abd al-Wadoud in recognition of al-Zarqawi— usually focuses on the situation in Algeria, but also expresses opinions on events in Libya, Mauritania, Morocco, and Tunisia.35

The tactics used by the group have also gone through some changes. Although AQIM has mainly used actions which are typical of the traditional guerrillas, including ambushes and attacks with mortars and rockets, since 2007 the group has begun using suicide attacks. In April of that year, a terrorist attack against a governmental building caused the death of 30 people. Months later, a double suicide attack caused 41 deaths including 17 United Nations workers. The group also sets off explosives when Algerian military forces drive by, a technique that analysts liken to the one used by the Taliban in Afghanistan. AQIM has claimed responsibility for other attacks against the military and Israeli and French interests in Mauritania. It has called for the Jihad against the military Government that took power in the country after the coup d'état in 2008. Furthermore, one of AQIM's tactics is the kidnapping of Westerners. This usually occurs in the Sahel, in the border region between Algeria and countries such as Mali, Niger and Mauritania. Kidnapping Westerners has two purposes: apply pressure to free the prisoners of Islamic movements, and obtain resources through the payment of ransom. Information on other sources of funding for the group is varied and include donations by followers, trafficking in arms, drugs, vehicles and tobacco through the Sahara Desert, which is a region of porous borders and difficult for authorities to control. This kind of activities has led some analysts to argue that AQIM looks more like a band that seeks economic benefit than a radical Jihadist group. However, these statements are countered by other specialists that believe the ideological bent of AQIM is visible in some of the group's most recent actions, for example, the execution of a British hostage when London refused to free a Jordanian cleric, last May, or the demand for the withdrawal of Italian troops from Afghanistan and Iraq in exchange of the liberation of two other hostages at the end of 2009.

US Intelligence sources believe that AQIM currently has between 300 and 400 combatants in a mountainous area east of Algiers and another 200 have a support role in the rest of the country. There are also speculations that the base of operations is in southern Algeria and northern Mali, and that some of the most recent actions attempted to demonstrate their capability to act in the entire Islamic Maghreb. Some analysts, nevertheless, indicate that the group moved its bases and sphere of action in response to the strategy rolled out by the

Algerian Government: on the one hand, a military offensive whose goal is to hound the group —with the belief that if they are busy surviving then they will not have time to prepare terrorist attacks— and, on the other, a campaign to question the legitimacy of AQIM's Islamic cause.36 Algiers has made it easy for former GPSC leaders to publicly request that their former colleagues abandon the armed struggle and is fostering Sufism, a branch of Islam associated with contemplation and not combat.37 In the current scenario, some analysts have also warned of the possibility that AQIM is trying to activate cells in Europe, especially after suspects of collaborating with the group have been arrested in several countries in the European Union. In this context, therefore, questions about the future of the group are also linked to the current and future initiatives of the EU and the US in the region and the effectiveness of the regional cooperation programs in Algeria, Mali, Mauritania and Niger in their struggle against AQIM.

America

Colombia

Start: 1964
Type: System
Internationalized internal
Main parties: Government, FARC, ELN, new paramilitary groups
Intensity: 3
Trend: =
Summary:
In 1964, in the context of a pact for alternating power between
the liberal and conservative parties (National Front), which
excluded any political alternatives, two armed opposition
movements emerged: the ELN (inspired by Che Guevara and
with support from the working classes and academics) and the
FARC (which had a peasants base and was influenced by Communist
ideals). During the 1970s, several other groups

emerged (M-19, EPL, etc.), which ended up negotiating with
the government and supporting a new Constitution (1991)
which established the bases for a Social State of Law. The end
of the 1980s saw the emergence of a number of paramilitary
self-defence groups instigated by sectors of the Armed Forces,
business people and politicians in defence of the status quo
and the maintenance of illegal businesses who promoted a
strategy of terror. Drug money is currently the main element
that keeps the war alive.
The unilateral liberation of political and military hostages
that the FARC have been carrying out little by little,
came to a stop when the Colombian Chief of Staff
demanded the rebels liberate all of the

hostages in exchange for nothing. Before the end of the year, however, the Government withdrew the request and authorized Senator Piedad Córdoba, the ICRC and the Catholic Church to continue efforts to achieve the freedom of another group of hostages. **In the southwestern region of the country the armed conflict intensified and the number of civilian and combatant victims rose dramatically, especially among the indigenous people,** which has been the main object of violence by members of the guerrillas, the paramilitary forces and state agents. The UN Special Rapporteur on Extrajudicial Executions in Colombia estimates that in the last three years nearly 2,000 people have been killed by members of the Armed Forces and presented as "guerrillas who have died in combat". This practice, known as "false positives", led to the dismissal, capture and trial of over one thousand troops. The **"cross-borderization" of the conflict caused a serious diplomatic incident between the Government of Colombia and those of Ecuador and Venezuela.** The situation deteriorated after the agreement between Colombian leader Álvaro Uribe with the Washington Government that allows US soldiers to use seven military bases (three air force, two naval and two army) on Colombian soil in operations against the guerrillas and drug trafficking. Other countries in the region, such as Brazil, Argentina and Bolivia, expressed their concern in the UNASUR summit for the growing interference of the US in South America with the pretext of supplying technical, logistical and intelligence support to the Colombian Government in their fight against the rebels.

Asia and Pacific

a) Southern Asia

Afghanistan

Start: 2001
Type: System
Internationalized internal
Main parties: Government, International Coalition (led by United States), ISAF (NATO), Taliban militia, warlords
Intensity: 3
Trend: ?
Summary:
The country has lived in almost constant armed

conflict since the invasion by Soviet troops in 1979, beginning a civil war between the Armed Forces (with Soviet support) and anti-Communist, Islamist guerrillas (Mujahideen). The withdrawal of Soviet troops in 1989 and the rise of the Mujahideen to power in 1992, in a context of chaos and internal fighting between the different anti-Communist factions, led to the emergence of the Taliban movement, which, at the end of the 1990s, controlled almost the entire Afghan territory. In November 2001, after the Al-Qaeda attacks of September 11, the US invaded the country and defeated the Taliban regime. After signing the Bonn agreements, an interim government was established led by Hamid Karzai and subsequently ratified at the polls.

Since 2006, there has been an escalation of violence in the country caused by the revival of the Taliban militias. **The year was marked by an increase of violence, controversy regarding the elections and the US announcement at the end of last year of a massive deployment of troops.** In the first eight months of the year 1,500 civilians died. Most of these deaths were attributed to the insurgency and a good number to international operations. The total death toll —combatants and civilians— at the end of the year reached several thousand. It was the most deadly year for the international troops, with 498 deaths, compared to 295 in 2008. **Combat became**

**more intense in the south, especially in the province of
Helmand**, where there was a wave of insurgent attacks,
especially during mid-year, in response to the international
operations. Insurgent violence became evident during the election campaign with at least thirty dead on
voting day. Especially serious were several international
air raids that caused numerous civilian deaths, such as
the US strike in Farah (southeast), with 97 civilians
dead according to the Afghan Government, or the one
launched by NATO in September in Kunduz, with 70
dead. For their part, the insurgency carried out attacks
in the capital, including a multiple attack in February
against several government organisms, leaving

twenty dead; an attack in October against a building where UN workers lived, with 11 dead, five of them UN workers; or an attack against the Indian embassy, with 17 dead.

Additionally, the United Nations and international NGOs alerted to the deteriorating situation of women.38 In this context of violence, at the end of the year, the US president announced a new strategy which included the deployment of 30,000 additional troops and a calendar for withdrawal which will begin in 2011. In this sense, the Taliban leader Mullah Omar rejected a negotiation with the Afghan Government as long as foreign troops were present.39 In the political sphere, the re-election of Hamid Karzai in the first round was annulled after hundreds of thousands of fraudulent votes were cancelled which favoured him. His rival, **Abdullah Abdullah, withdrew from the second round and denounced the lack of guarantees. Karzai was declared the winner without having to go a second round** which had an impact on the legitimacy of the process.

India (Assam)
Start: 1983
Type: Self-government, Identity
Internationalized internal
Main parties: Government, ULFA, DHD, Black Widow, NDFB
Intensity: 2
Trend: =
Sintesis:
The ULFA armed opposition group emerged in

1979 with the aim of freeing the state of Assam from Indian colonisation and establishing a sovereign State. The demographic transformations the state underwent after the partition of the Indian subcontinent, with the arrival of two million people from Bangladesh, are at the centre of the ethnic Assamese population's demands for recognition of their cultural and civil rights and the establishment of an independent State. During the 1980s and 1990s several escalations of violence occurred as well as attempts at negotiation which failed. A peace process began in 2005 that resulted in a decrease in violence, but was interrupted in 2006, giving rise to a new escalation of the conflict. Additionally, during the 1980s armed groups of

Bodo origin emerged, such as the NDFB, and demanded recognition of their identity as opposed to the majority Assamese population

38. See Chapter 6 (Gender).
39. See Chapter 3 (Peace processes).

Armed Conflicts **37**

Overall, violence remained at a level comparable to previous years, with at least 380 deaths in the state of Assam between January and mid-December, although **the confl ict with the Dimasa armed group "Black Widow" was escalated, which forced the group to surrender**. After months of insurgent violence and military operations against Black Widow in the North Cachar Hills district, a government ultimatum in September with the threat of a large scale offensive brought about the surrender

of the group. Nearly 400 members were transferred
to cantonment sites. In the first nine months of the year, at least one hundred people died due to violence
in the district which caused the displacement of thousands of people and mainly affected the Dimasa
and Zeme Naga populations. After their surrender, some
media organizations reported that other irregular groups
were committing acts of violence due to the insurgent
power vacuum created. Moreover, with regard to the
ULFA conflict, the group **continued to be active during**
the year and the Police held them responsible for several
attacks, including several explosions in January in
Guwahati that caused fifty deaths and 60 wounded;

various multiple explosions in April, also in Guwahati,
with a dozen dead and 80 wounded; and two explosions
in Nalbarri in November with nearly a dozen deaths and
over 50 wounded. The group denied responsibility for
the attacks **and in November agreed to the possibility of
beginning peace talks with the Government** which coincided
with civilian calls for dialogue.40 In connection with the NDFB Bodo confl ict, the Administration extended
the ceasefi re agreement and began peace talks with
the group in Delhi, but maintained military operations
against the faction led by Ranjan Daimary.41

India (Jammu and Kashmir)
Start: 1989
Type: Self-government, Identity
Internationalized internal

Main parties: Government, JKLF, Lashkar-e-Tayyeba, Hizbul Mujahideen
Intensity: 2
Trend: ?
Summary:
The armed conflict in the Indian state of Jammu and Kashmir has its origin in the dispute over the region of Kashmir which has set India and Pakistan against each other since their independence and partition. On three occasions (1947-1948; 1965; 1971) the two countries have clashed in armed conflict, both claiming sovereignty over the region, which is split between India, Pakistan and China. The armed conflict between India and Pakistan in 1947 gave rise to the current division and creation of a *de facto* border between the two countries. Since 1989, the armed conflict has

moved to the interior of the state of Jammu and Kashmir, where a multitude of insurgent groups, in favour of full independence for the state or unconditional adhesion to Pakistan, confront the Indian security forces. Since the beginning of the peace process between India and Pakistan in 2004, violence has declined considerably, although the armed groups remain active. Around 365 people died in 2009, which was slightly below the figure for previous years. In this sense, **the Government stated on several occasions that the conflict was in a sustained period of decrease in violence** and announced that it intended to withdraw thousands of troops from Jammu and Kashmir to redeploy them in areas where the CPI-M armed Maoist group operates. Nevertheless, in December the Government had only withdrawn 15.000 troops and had not announced the number of soldiers involved or a calendar for withdrawal. Meanwhile, the Government declared that only 110 of the 3,429 missing people in the region between 1990 and 2009 had disappeared after being arrested by the State security forces. However, **human rights organizations demanded a truth commission be set up since they considered that the number of missing persons could be as high as 8,000, the majority after being arrested by the State security forces.** Apart from the fighting that took place near the Line of Control, which caused the majority of the deaths, there were massive protests at different times of the year against the presence and the *modus operandi* of the security forces in Jammu and Kashmir. During the protests, led by pro-independence organizations such as Hurriyat Conference or United Jihad Council, hundreds of people were wounded and a similar number arrested. Political and social tension climbed signifi cantly at certain times during the year, such as during the legislative elections in April and May (boycotted by some organizations) or the commemoration of India's independence in the month of August. In addition, in the second and third quarters massive protests were held for the rape and murder of two women, allegedly by the State security forces.

India (Manipur)

Start: 1982
Type: Self-government, Identity
Internal
Main parties: Government, PLA, UNLF, PREPAK, KNF, KNA, KYKL
Intensity: 2
Trend: ?
Summary:
The armed conflict that confronts the government with various armed groups operating in the state, as well as some who are fighting against each other, began with demands for independence by several of these groups, and with the tensions that exist between the different ethnic groups that coexist in the

state. In the 1960s and 1970s various armed groups emerged, some inspired by Communism and others of ethnic origin. These groups have remained active throughout the subsequent decades. In addition, the regional context of a state which shares borders with Nagaland, Assam and Myanmar also marked the development of conflict in Manipur, and tensions between Manipuri ethnic groups and the Naga population are constant. The economic impoverishment of the state and its isolation from the rest of the country have decisively contributed to reinforcing a feeling of injustice among the Manipuri population.

40. See Chapter 3 (Peace processes).
41. Figure provided by the SATP think tank. The mortality data for the different confl icts in India

and Pakistan are from the same source, in <http://www.satp.org/default.asp>.

[38] Alert 2010

Fighting continued between the security forces and the different armed groups, with some 380 deaths, one hundred less than the previous year. In the second half of the year armed violence decreased while social and political tension were on the rise. The insurgency was especially active in the Thoubal and Imphal districts. In Imphal, the murder of several civil servants in February, allegedly by the NSCN-IM (from the neighbouring state of Nagaland), brought on the imposition of a curfew which continued until the end of March. Moreover, in the Bishnupur district, the Police and Assam Rifles security force launched a special counterinsurgency operation in April which caused dozens of casualties in the armed groups of the area, mainly in the PREPAK. Beginning in July, violence in the state declined although social tension was on the rise with massive demonstrations which combined strikes and protests organized by the major Naga organizations and numerous civil society groups, as well as protests by the political opposition. They all **demanded the resignation of the state prime minister, Okram Singh, for the over 210 murders allegedly committed by the security forces and disguised as combat casualties**. The protests were sparked by the death, in July, of a young activist who was in favour of independence —according to some sectors he was killed in police custody—, and because of the denouncement of an increase in the number of murders that allegedly were being covered up. During the year there were also civilian protests against the intimidation and threats from armed groups. In addition, the agreement was again renewed for another year to suspend hostilities between the central Government, the Government of Manipur and two Kuki armed groups, the Kuki National Organisation and the United People's Front.

India (Nagaland)
Start: 1955

Type: Self-government, Identity
Internal
Main parties: Government, NSCN-K, NSCN-IM
Intensity: 1
Trend: Fin
Summary:
El The conflict that affects the state of Nagaland began after
the British decolonization process in India (1947) when a
Naga movement emerged demanding recognition for the collective
rights of the population, mostly Christian, as opposed
to the majority which are Indian Hindu. The founding of the
NCC Naga organization in 1946 marks the beginning of political
demands for independence for the Naga people. These
demands evolved over the following decades both in content
(Nagaland independence or the creation of the Great Nagaland

including territories from neighbouring states inhabited
by Nagas) and in the methods of opposition, with the beginning
of the armed struggle in 1955. In 1980 the NSCN armed
opposition group was created as a result of disagreements with
more moderate political groups, and eight years later split into
two factions, Isaac Muivah and Khaplang. Since 1997 the
NSCN-IM has maintained a ceasefire agreement and talks
with the Indian Government, but in recent years the number of
clashes between the two groups has multiplied. **Violence in the state declined signifi cantly during the
year,** compared to the increase in fi ghting and number
of victims during the 2007 and 2008 confl ict, and was
therefore no longer considered an armed confl

ict beginning in the first quarter.42 Even so, some incidents during the first quarter were reported. On the one hand, there were clashes between the State security forces and the NSCN-IM, which warned the Government that it would not tolerate the presence of security forces in the area around the camps where its members are stationed. On the other hand, fighting took place between the NSCN-IM and rival NSCN-K in the area of Bhandari, in the Wokha district. Additionally, in February in the neighbouring state of Manipur, the murder of three Government employees by members of the **NSCN-IM** created tension between the parties in the conflict,

although the armed group considered the attack the
responsibility of individuals and requested that it not be
used to hamper the peace process.43
Moreover, **the group's leader, Isaac Chisi Swu, reasserted his commitment
to a peaceful solution to the confl ict.**

India (CPI-M)
Start: 1967
Type: System
Internal
Main parties: Government, CPI-M (Naxalites)
Intensity: 2
Trend: ⁈
Summary:
The armed conflict in which confronts the Indian government
with the CPI-M Maoist armed group (known as the Naxalites,
in honour of the town where the movement was created)
affects numerous Indian states. The CPI-M

surfaced in West Bengal at the end of the 1960s with demands related to the eradication of the land ownership system, as well as strong criticism of the system of parliamentary democracy, which was considered as a colonial legacy. Since then, armed activity has been constant and has been accompanied by the establishment of parallel systems of government in the areas under its control, which are mainly rural. Military operations against this group, considered by the Indian government as a terrorist organization, have been constant. In 2004, a negotiation process began which ended in failure. **Violence climbed, reaching 960 deaths during the year.** The most signifi cant increase was in the states of Chhattishgarh,

West Bengal and Jharkhand where the most violent clashes were reported, as opposed to Orissa where there was a decline. During the year there were Naxalite attacks which caused a high number of deaths, the one in Chhattishgarh in June being the most notable with 39 police casualties and 15 wounded. This was the largest number of victims in one single day since the beginning of the conflict. Moreover, the insurgency used a large number of combatants in some of the attacks, such as the one against the Police in Maharashtra with 200 insurgents and 17 police dead; or another offensive against the Police in the state of Bihar with 200 insurgents that caused the death of 10 police officers. In addition, **the**

42. See Chapter 2 (Socio-political crises).
43. See Chapter 3 (Peace processes).

state West Bengal was, for the first time, the scene for high levels of violence. In this state there were over one hundred deaths during the year, compared to 20 in 2008, in fighting set off by the deployment of 1,800 soldiers in the area in June and after the death of 10 members of the government party, the CPI-M (this party has the same name as the armed group, but is opposed to it). In recent months, tension had mounted in the area of Lalgarh, which is mostly under Naxalite control since the end of 2008 when the Police were expelled and part of the State administration was dismantled. The violence in West Bengal

caused the displacement of thousands of civilians.
In the third quarter the authorities regained political and military control. Given the existing violence in the country, **seven states supported the initiative of the Interior Minister to coordinate the counterinsurgency campaign in the border regions.** Furthermore, in October a new strategy was announced, headed by the Police in the different states and which included the deployment of 70,000 members
of the security forces, elite commandos and special forces,
and the use of the Air Force. This plan was heavily
criticized by the civil society. This operation was launched
in December, known as Green Hunt, with the transfer of
3,000 police agents from Jammu and Kashmir to Chhattisgarh.
The launch coincided with a leak that the insurgency

was approaching the Indian capital.

Pakistan (Baluchistan)

Start: 2005
Type: Self-government, Resources
Internal
Main parties: Government, BLA, BRA and BLF
Intensity: 2
Trend: =
Summary:
Since the creation of the State of Pakistan in 1947, Baluchistan,
the richest province in natural resources but with
some of the highest poverty rates in the country, has experienced
four periods of armed violence (1948, 1958, 1963-69
and 1973-77) in which the insurgents have spelled out their
objective of achieving greater autonomy or even independence.
In 2005, the armed insurgency reappeared on the
scene, mainly attacking gas extraction

infrastructures. The BLA armed opposition group became the main force opposing the presence of the central Government, which it accused of taking advantage of the wealth of the province without any of this benefiting the local population. As a consequence of the resurgence of the armed opposition, a military operation was launched in the province in 2005, causing the displacement of the civilian population and armed confrontations.

Conflict related violence in the region of Baluchistan was similar to levels in 2008. **The year began with the announcement by the BLA, BRA and BLF opposition armed groups that they were suspending the ceasefire that they had unilaterally declared at the end**

of 2008.
The argument used was the need to respond to the Armed Forces offensive which they accused of killing 50 people during the ceasefi re. During this period the insurgency had continued their attacks and, therefore, the decision to renew the armed struggle was just the continuation of a situation of violence that, in practice, had been maintained in the region. Following the pattern established since violence was renewed in 2005, the opposition groups' actions concentrated on infrastructures, rail networks and gas pipelines, as well as bombings against the security forces. In addition, kidnappings were carried out which resulted in the death of dozens of hostages. In parallel, **throughout**

the year nationalist Baluchi leaders were murdered, which was attributed to the security forces. On several occasions these deaths sparked massive protests and strikes that, in turn, caused more fatalities and dozens of wounded. In September, the Government announced a general amnesty for Baluchi political prisoners and reported that the accusations of disappearances and torture of activists in the province were being investigated by the Pakistani Human Rights Commission. In December, according to official estimates, one thousand people were missing. At the end of the year, the Government presented a plan in the Parliament to increase the autonomy of Baluchistan, but the proposal was considered insufficient and rejected. On the regional level, Islamabad accused Afghanistan and India of providing support for the insurgency in

Baluchistan, which is the poorest province in Pakistan
in spite of its abundant natural resources. Both Governments rejected these accusations.

Pakistan (northwest)

Start: 2001
Type: System
Internationalized internal
Main parties: Government, Taliban militias, tribal
militias, US
Intensity: 3
Trend: ?
Summary:
The armed conflict in the northwest region of the country
began as part of the armed conflict in Afghanistan after the
US bombings in 2001. The area is made up of the Federally
Administered Tribal Areas (FATA), which had been inaccessible
to the Pakistani Government until 2002, when the first

military operations began in the area – and the North-West
Frontier Province (NWFP). After the fall of the Taliban regime
in Afghanistan at the end of 2001, members of the Taliban
militias with alleged connections to al-Qaeda, took refuge in
this area, giving rise to large-scale military operations by the
Pakistani Armed Forces (nearly 50,000 soldiers have been
deployed) with US support. The local population, largely
from the Pashtun ethnic group, have been accused of supporting
the combatants from Afghanistan. Since the first
operations in 2002, violence has been on the rise.
**The atmosphere of violence in the northwest got worse,
with at least 2,800 deaths during the year** and had a

greater effect on the NWFP during the first half of the
year and on the FATA in the final months. In February
in the NWFP, the central Government accepted an
agreement between the provincial Government and the
Tehrik-e-Nifaz-e-Shariah Mohammadi organization,

The conflict in northwest Pakistan between the Taliban militia and the Army became worse, with over 2,800 deaths and hundreds of thousands of displaced persons

which included the application of Islamic law in some
areas of the province, disarmament of the militias and

the end to military operations. This was followed by a ceasefire in Swat. Nevertheless, violence returned shortly after, with the **Taliban expansion in the former Malakand division** (Swat, Dir, Malakand and Buner districts, among others), and reached Buer and Dir, **only one hundred kilometers from Islamabad.** Counteroffensive operations by the Army in April forced the Taliban to retreat and put an end to the talks. According to UNHCR, since the beginning of operations in the NWFP, 2.3 million people have been displaced because of the violence.44 More than one thousand people died in these actions and the Pakistani prime minister declared the area a disaster zone. The Government announced in July that it had regained control, although throughout the rest of the year the NWFP continued to be the scene of clashes and suicide attacks which caused hundreds of deaths. This included **an attack on a market in Peshawar with 96 fatalities, the deadliest in Pakistan in the last two years**, and which coincided with a visit by the US Secretary of State Hillary Clinton. Furthermore, the situation in the FATA deteriorated considerably after the peace agreement between the insurgency and the authorities failed in June. This led to more violence with large scale military offensives and a rise in insurgent attacks in areas such as Khyber in

September, which caused tens of thousands of displaced
people and over one hundred victims, and South
Waziristan since October, with over 600 dead and hundreds
of thousands of displaced people. In addition, **attacks by unmanned US drones caused dozens of deaths.** The death of Baitullah Mehsud, leader of the
TTP, in an attack by the US was reported in August.

Sri Lanka (northeast)
Start: 1983
Type: Self-government, Identity
Internal
Main parties: Government, LTTE
Intensity: 3
Trend: Fin
Summary:
In 1983, the Tamil pro-independence armed opposition group,
the LTTE, began the armed conflict that has

ravaged Sri Lanka for the past three decades. After the decolonisation of the island in 1948, the growing marginalisation of the Tamil population by the Government, which is mostly made up of the Sinhalese elite, led the group to fight for the establishment of an independent Tamil State. Since 1983, each of the three phases of the conflict has ended with a failed peace process.

In 2002, peace negotiations began once again with Norwegian mediation, following the signing of a ceasefire agreement. The failure of the talks sparked a violent renewal of the armed conflict in 2006. In May 2009, the Armed Forces inflicted a military defeat on the LTTE and regained control over the entire country after killing the armed group's leader, Velupillai Prabhakaran. In May, **President Mahinda Rajapakse declared that the armed conflict**, which had lasted 26 years and caused 86,000 deaths, **had ended**. Since then, the levels of violence have dropped drastically and this context is now no longer considered an armed conflict. 45 The Armed Forces' final offensive on the remaining LTTE strongholds began in January with the capture of Kilinochchi, where the group's headquarters had been located in recent years, and the Jaffna peninsula. Soon after, in February, the Army took the city of Mullaitivu and the Chalai naval base which significantly weakened

the group's military capabilities and cornered them into
a small area of the territory. According to Government
sources, in the previous 34 months of the armed confl ict
nearly 22,000 insurgents and died and 6,200 soldiers.
Conversely, the **United Nations stated that about 7,000
civilians had died and another 14,000 had been wounded
between the months of January and May 2009**. In
this sense, **the United Nations High Commissioner for
Human Rights, Navi Pillay, denounced that both sides
could have committed war crimes** in the fi nal stages of
the armed confl ict: the Government for bombing areas
designated to protect civilians and for using cluster

bombs, and the LTTE for using civilians as human shields and for blocking the evacuation of the civilian population in areas under its control. The land, air and sea battles in the final weeks of the Army's offensive forced the displacement of approximately 300,000 people with the majority being trapped in the combat areas.

Finally, the Government officially declared an end to the armed conflict the day after the death of the LTTE leader, Velupillai Prabhakaran, was confirmed.

b) Southeast Asia and Oceania

Philippines (NPA)

Start: 1969
Type: System
Internal
Main parties: Government, NPA
Intensity: 1

Trend: =

Summary:

The NPA, the armed wing of the Communist Party of the Philippines, began its armed struggle in 1969 and reached its peak in the 1980s, during the dictatorship of Ferdinand Marcos. Although the group was seriously weakened at the beginning of the 1990s —because of internal purges, the democratisation of the Philippines during the second half of the 1980s and an offering of an amnesty–, it is currently estimated that the NPA operates in most of the country's provinces. After the September 11, 2001 attacks, the NPA was included in the US and EU terrorist organization lists, which greatly undermined the trust between both parties and to a large extent caused the

peace talks with Gloria Macapagal Arroyo's Government to be
broken off. The political arm of the NPA, whose main aim is to
take power and transform the political and socio-economic
system, are the Communist Party of the Philippines and the
National Democratic Front (NDF), which brings together various
Communist-inspired organisations.

44. See Chapter 4 (Humanitarian crises).
45. See Chapter 2 (Socio-political crises).

Armed Conflicts **41**

Despite continuing contacts between the Government
and the NDF to renew the peace process,49 fighting took
place in many provinces throughout the year. Moreover,
the Government insisted on its plan to defeat the NPA
by 2010, as the President had repeated on several

occasions. In this sense, **the Government substantially increased the number of military units dedicated to fight the NPA and reinforced the demobilization and reintegration program for combatants**. Manila reported that since the program began in 2001, over 12,000 insurgents, especially from the NPA, had accepted to participate in it and 3,700 members of the NPA had surrendered since 2004. Violence rose three times during the year. First, in the month of April, coinciding with the commemoration of the 40th anniversary of the founding of the armed group and with the joint military exercises that the Philippine and US troops conduct each year. At different times of the year the NPA also carried out several attacks on US troops that were realizing counter-terrorism tasks in Mindanao. Second, violence rose again in September, shortly after an attempt to renew the peace process failed. Finally, in November and December, over 40 people died in different clashes which were especially intense in Mindanao. The Government accused the NPA of setting off more and more bombs by remote control and of increasing their attacks on the civilian population. In this sense, the Government reported that between May 2008 and May 2009 the NPA had murdered over 120 people accused of providing information to the

Government or
not paying the revolutionary tax. The NPA denied this
information and accused the Army of militarizing the
civilian population with the creation of self-defence
groups to fi ght against the NPA.

Philippines (Mindanao-MILF)

Start: 1978
Type: Self-government, Identity
Internal
Main parties: Government, MILF
Intensity: 2
Trend: ?
Summary:
The armed conflict in Mindanao dates back to the end of the
1960s, when Nur Misuari founded the MNLF to fight for the
self-determination of the Moro people –a number of Islamized
ethnolinguistic groups that are politically organised into independent

sultanates since the 15th century–. The MILF, for
strategic, ideological and leadership reasons, broke away from
the MNLF at the end of the 1970s and continued with the
armed struggle while the MNLF signed a peace agreement in
1996 which included a certain degree of autonomy for the
areas of Mindanao that are mostly Muslim (Autonomous Region
in Muslim Mindanao). Despite the fact that both parties signed

46. There is no agreement on the exact number of combatants. After the end of the conflict, the Government has stated that approximately 10,000
people remain under arrest accused of having links to the armed group. Moreover, the Government affirmed that the number of insurgents killed
in the 34 month period prior to the defeat of the armed group was 22,000 (BBC. "Colombo to

rehabilitate rebels", BBC, 27 May 2009, in <http://news.bbc.co.uk/2/hi/south_asia/8069469.stm>.

47. The United Kingdom considered the LTTE a terrorist group since 2000 and the US named it Specially Designated Global Terrorist since November 2001.

48. It is estimated that before 2000 the Diaspora provided approximately 50 million dollars yearly. Byman, Daniel, Peter Chalk, Bruce Hoffman, William Rosenau and David Brannan. *Trends in Outside Support for Insurgent Movements*. Santa Monica: RAND, 2001.

49. See Chapter 3 (Peace processes).

Box 1.2. **The reasons behind the military defeat of the LTTE**

On May 19, 2009, the president of Sri Lanka, Mahinda Rajapakse, announced the military defeat of the Tamil armed opposition group LTTE after having killed its leader, Vellupillai Prabakharan. The defeat of one of the most powerful insurgencies in

the world –approximately 15,000 combatants,46 army, air force, navy and important financial resources– and for 26 years able
to corner the Armed Forces, raised many questions regarding the key to an unforeseen victory. Although the ultimate reasons
for the defeat are still not clear, a multi-causal approach seems necessary to attempt to explain how the Government was able
to regain control of the entire island of Sri Lanka and dismantle the LTTE.

First, it is necessary to mention the split by Coronel Karuna and the impact it had on the group, which meant losing control
of the east of the island and the desertion of an important number of LTTE combatants. Around 6,000 combatants left the
ranks of the LTTE to join Karuna. The support provided by this faction to the Armed Forces in 2006 and 2007 was the beginning
of the armed group's decline, which at that time was mainly grouped in the north of the island.

Second, the LTTE defeat

can also be included in the context of the global war against terrorism. In fact, the armed group was included in the terrorist organizations list of the EU and Canada in 2006.47 The inclusion of the LTTE in the list not only hampered the negotiation process between the Sri Lankan Government and the armed organization because it forbade its leaders from travelling to UE countries, but also was a setback in logistic and financial terms since it made it more difficult to gain access to the economic resources provided by the diaspora. Furthermore, contributions by the diaspora – vital for the armed group's maintenance–48 had dwindled in recent years. Among the reasons analysts give for the growing distance between the diaspora and the armed group are certain practices (recruitment of child soldiers, utilization of the civilian population) and the fact that the group was self-proclaimed as the only legitimate representative of the Tamil people, which excluded other Tamil voices that were critical of the armed group's methods. Finally, the Government's determination to achieve a military victory no matter what the cost should be mentioned. This led them to give priority to military goals over other issues such as protecting the civilian population and respecting International Humanitarian Law. The end result was that the victory was accompanied by grave human rights violations, such as extrajudicial executions or bombings in areas set aside for the civilian population.

42 Alert 2010

a ceasefire in 2003 (monitored by an international mission) and that in recent years several rounds of negotiations have been held with the Government –with help from Malaysia and focusing on the ancestral territories of the Moro people– the MILF continues to be active in several regions of Mindanao and it is estimated to have around 11,000 members.

Although the intensity of the conflict declined compared to the last quarter of 2008, fighting continued throughout the year. The Government declared that one hundred members of the MILF had died during the fighting in January, in which the Army had conducted air strikes and had about 50 casualties in its own ranks. These clashes, especially those that took place in the provinces of Sultan Kudarat and Maguindanao, caused the displacement of thousands of people. **Manila indicated that in the month of February over 120 people had died due to the precarious conditions in the displacement centres**. In subsequent months the Army stepped up its campaign to arrest those allegedly responsible for the outbreak of violence that took place in Mindanao in the final third of 2008, such as the commander Ameril Umbra Kato. The exact number of people that died during this offensive is unknown, although the Armed Forces announced that one hundred insurgents had died in the month of June alone, and a minimum of 200 combatants had surrendered. Conversely, **the MILF declared that over 500 soldiers had died between August 2008 and July 2009.** The Government accused the MILF of continuing to attack the civilian population and of participating in dozens of attacks with explosive devices. The MILF accused the Government of conducting air strikes and systematically

destroying the populations' homes. According to
official sources, in the first months of the year alone
over 2,000 homes had been burned in the province of
Maguindanao. Fighting decreased significantly during
the second half of the year due to the signing of several
agreements between the parties,50 although isolated
incidents continued to take place (such as the alleged
participation of MILF members in the kidnapping of an
Irish priest in October or the attack on a prison in
Basilan in December), insurgent leaders were arrested
and sporadic violations of the ceasefire agreement
occurred.

Philippines (Mindanao-Abu Sayyaf)

Start: 1991
Type: Self-government, Identity, System
Internationalized internal
Main parties: Government, Abu Sayyaf
Intensity: 1
Trend: ?
Summary:
The Abu Sayyaf group has been fighting since the 1990s to
establish an independent Islamic state in the Sulu archipelago
and the western regions of Mindanao (south). It initially
recruited disaffected members from other armed groups, such
as the MILF or the MNLF. However, it subsequently distanced
itself ideologically from both organisations and became more
systematically involved in kidnappings, extortion, decapitation
and bomb attacks, thus being included in the US and EU lists
of terrorist organisations. The Government

considers that its counterinsurgency strategy in recent years has significantly weakened the leadership and military capability of the group. It also warns, however, that Abu Sayyaf continues to be a threat to the State because of the significant resources that it obtains through kidnapping and through alleged alliances with organisations considered as terrorists, such as Al-Qaeda or Jemaah Islamiyah. Fighting rose appreciably compared to last year and has caused the death of close to 200 people. The first part of the year was marked by an Armed Forces operation to free the hostages in Abu Sayyaf's hands, especially the three workers from the International Committee of the Red

Cross (two of them foreigners) who had been kidnapped
in January. Fighting was especially intense in July and
caused the death of over 50 people and the displacement
of some 10,000 people on Jolo Island. A few days after
the last Red Cross worker was set free, the Armed Forces
increased their military pressure against the group and
deployed thousands of additional soldiers in the Sulu Archipelago.
Thus, **in mid-August, 54 people, 23 of them soldiers, died on Basilan Island in one of the fiercest clashes in recent years.** A few weeks later, at the beginning
of September, 34 members of Abu Sayyaf and eight
soldiers died during the taking of one of the group's main
camps on Jolo Island in which the Army used air

strikes.
The Armed Forces declared that both the military offensive during the last year and several internal purges had enormously weakened the armed capability of Abu Sayyaf, although they recognized that the group was trying to rebuild its links with organizations in the Middle East and, also, that each year it obtained large amounts of income from the kidnappings. In this sense, **Manila indicated that Abu Sayyaf had captured over 200 people since 2003**. Furthermore, the Government said the group was responsible for most of the 140 attacks with explosive devices during the year which killed over 50 people and wounded almost 300. Finally, the Government

warned again of the presence of foreign organizations considered terrorists that operate in the south of the country and maintain close ties to Abu Sayyaf.

Myanmar

Start: 1948
Type: Self-government, Identity
Internal
Main parties: Government, armed groups (KNU/KNLA, SSA-S, KNPP, UWSA, CNF, ALP, DKBA, KNPLAC, SSNPLO)
Intensity: 1
Trend: ?
Summary:
Since 1948, dozens of armed insurgent groups of ethnic origin have confronted the government of Myanmar to demand recognition of their distinct ethnic and cultural characteristics and call for reforms in the territorial structure

of the State or independence. Since the beginning of the military dictatorship in 1962, the Armed Forces have been combating armed groups in the ethnic states. These groups combine demands

50. See Chapter 3 (Peace processes).

for self-determination for minorities and calls for democratisation, a goal they share with the political opposition. In 1988, the Government launched a ceasefire process with part of the insurgent groups which allowed them to continue with their economic activity (mainly, trafficking in drugs and precious stones). Nevertheless, military operations have been constant for decades and have been especially aimed at the civilian population to force the displacement of hundreds of thousands of people with the intention of eliminating the armed groups' bases.

The two main scenes of violence were the states of Karen and Shan, although attacks with explosive devices were also reported in Rangoon and Mon State. In Karen state, the Armed Forces and the Karen armed group DKBA (split off from the KNU) conducted the most important military offensive of the decade which forced 4,000 people to flee to Thailand. Some voices indicated that the motivation for the offensive was an attempt by the DKBA to militarily eradicate the KNU bases, control the region's natural resources and maintain

greater commercial ties with neighbouring Thailand. In addition, **the DKBA began a forcible recruitment campaign among the civilian population in Karen state** to increase its forces from 6,000 to 9,000 and thus meet Government requirements for joining the border patrol, which is under the Armed Forces. The number of people that died during the fighting is unknown, although the KNU declared that some 250 soldiers could have died during the first half of the year. In turn,
Thailand increased pressure on the KNU to restrict its
armed activity in Thai territory. In Shan state, sporadic
clashes took place between the Army and the armed
groups SSA-S, KNPP and PNLO. **In July and August, over 30,000 people were forced to cross the border with China due to the fighting between the Armed Forces**

and the MNDAA, which was aided by the UWSA. Since mid-2008, tension in this state has increased notably between the Government and several armed groups –like the KIA, the NDAA or the SSA-N– that signed ceasefire agreements with the Government but refuse to join the border patrol. In this sense, several sources warned about growing military tension between the Government and the UWSA (the most powerful armed group) and of the possible renewal of a high intensity conflict in Shan or Kachin states, where the KIO has also warned that it may renew armed activity if the Government obliges them to join the border patrol.

Thailand (South)

Start: 2004
Type: Self-government, Identity
Internal
Main parties: Government, secessionist armed opposition groups
Intensity: 2
Trend: =
Summary:

The conflict in southern Thailand dates back to the beginning
of the 20th century, when the then Kingdom of Siam and the
British colonial government in the Malay peninsula decided to
divide up the Sultanate of Patani, leaving some territories
under the sovereign control of current day Malaysia and others
(the southern provinces of Songkhla, Yala, Patani and Narathiwat)
under Thai control. During the 20th century groups have
existed that fought to resist political cultural

and religious homogenization driven by Bangkok or to demand the independence of these provinces with a Malay-Muslim majority. The conflict reached its peak in the 1960s and 1970s and tapered off thanks to the democratization of the country. Nevertheless, the arrival to power of Thaksin Shinawatra in 2001 resulted in a drastic change of direction in the counterinsurgency policies and preceded the armed conflict which affects the region since 2004. The civilian population, both Buddhist and Muslim, is the main victim of the violence. Normally, no groups take responsibility for the actions. **The Government declared that violence was falling in the fi rst months of 2009, but a study by the Thai** research centre Deep South Watch presented in mid-September revealed that although levels of violence had gradually decreased since 2007 they had been on the rise again in 2009 and had reached 100 armed incidents per month (the highest number since 2007). The centre pointed out that from 2004 to August 2009 over 9,000 armed incidents had taken place, 3,600 people had died and over 6,000 had been wounded. Some media outlets, however, consider that the number of fatalities has surpassed 4,000 since 2004. As in previous years, the violence mainly affected the civilian population (Buddhist and Muslim) with a considerable impact on the educational domain, with dozens of attacks on schools and teachers. Intelligence sources estimate that the insurgency, led mainly by the BRN-C

group, currently has between 4,000 and 9,000 active
members which operate in small independent cells and
have considerable autonomy to act. Although the
Government declared that the key to resolving the
armed confl ict was to drive development projects,
strengthen cooperation with Malaysia, increase local
participation and carry out educational and cultural
measures, **Bangkok increased its military presence in
the south of the country (where almost half of the Army
is already deployed) and extended the state of emergency
in the three southern provinces.** In this sense,
while Amnesty International accused the Armed Forces
of systematically practicing torture, several

organizations meanwhile criticized the Government for promoting the creation of civilian self-defence groups.

Europe

Russia (Chechnya)

Start: 1999

Type: Self-government, Identity, System
Internal

Main parties: Russian Federal Government, Government of Chechnya, armed opposition groups

Intensity: 1

Trend: ?

Summary:

After the so-called first Chechen war (1994-1996) which confronted the Russian Federation with the Republic of Chechnya,

The Myanmar Armed Forces conducted one of the fiercest counterinsurgency offensives in recent

years in Karen state

44 Alert 2010

Summary:

The low-level violence experienced in Ingushetia since the beginning of the 21st century confronts the local and federal security forces with a network of armed Islamist cells known as the Jamaat Ingush and is part of the Caucasus Front (movement that brings together the different insurgent groups in the northern Caucasus). With origins that date back to the participation of Ingush fighters in the first Chechen War (1994-1996), since 2002 the Ingush insurgency has been restructured along territorial lines and has promoted a campaign of local violence. Without the nationalist drive of Chechnya, it pursues the establishment of an Islamic state in the Caucasus. The beginning of violence in Ingushetia occurred during the presidency in the Republic of Murat Zyazikov, whose term (2002-2008) is said to have been responsible for human rights violations, corruption, poverty, social and political tension and an atmosphere of misgovernment. The Ingush insurgents periodically attack military and civilian personnel belonging to the Russian and local state machinery. 2008 marked an increase in violence and tension. **The security situation in the Republic continued to deteriorate, in spite of a change in the Presidency** at the end of 2008 and the announcement by the new leader, Yunus-bek Yevkurov, of his willingness to dialogue with the Islamic insurgency. During the year over one hundred people died, including insurgents, members of the security forces and civilians. The BBC estimated the number at 200 at the end of October and the NGO Médecins Sans Frontières had reported 140 during the first six months of the year. Additionally, suicide attacks and selective attacks by the insurgency against high level officials increased. In of the most notable incidents, **25 people died and 140 were wounded, including children, in a suicide attack with a truck bomb** against a police complex in the city of Nazran in August. This was the most deadly attack in the North Caucasus in recent years. The **Ingush president was also the victim**

of an attack, in which he was wounded. In different attacks during the year high level offi cials died, such as the Minister of Construction and the deputy head of the Supreme Court. In response, Ingushetia and Chechnya increased their counterinsurgency cooperation. Meanwhile, the atmosphere of violence and abuses against the civilian population continued. The NGO Memorial warned that the war against terrorism in the North Caucasus had turned into a state of terror due to **extrajudicial executions, torture, disappearances and impunity**, also present in Ingushetia. The Ingush political opponent, Maksharip Aushev, was killed in the neighbouring republic of Kabardino-Balkaria. In October, **the president dismissed the entire Government** and criticized them for not having suitable strategies to resolve the Republic's socio-economic problems. Furthermore, he began contacts with local clans to create a council of *teips* (clans) to address Ingushetia's problems. mainly over the issue of the latter's independence (which was unilaterally proclaimed during the break-up of the USSR), and which ended in a peace treaty that failed to resolve Chechnya's status, the conflict resumed in 1999 in what became known as the second Chechen war and was set off triggered by incursions into Dagestan by Chechen rebels and attacks on Russian cities.

Prior to elections and using anti-terrorist rhetoric, the Russian military once again entered Chechnya to combat the moderate pro-independence regime that had emerged following the first war and that had itself been victim of internal disputes and growing criminality. Russia announced the end of the war in 2001, without having achieved any agreement or a definitive victory, and promoted a statute of autonomy and a pro-Russian Chechen administration. However, fighting continued accompanied by a growing Islamization of the Chechen rebel troops and the regionalization of the armed struggle. There was a clear contrast between the offi cial rhetoric of stability and a deteriorating security situation, especially for the civilian population. In mid-April, the Kremlin announced the **end to the anti-terrorism operation**

in Chechnya in reference to the military campaign
began in 1999 which gave rise to the second Chechen
war. The decision implies the end to special measures
and the withdrawal of temporary federal troops. In spite
of the announcement, **violence rose during the year with
an increase of actions by the irregular units, including
suicide attacks.** Over one hundred people died in 2009
due to insurgent and counterinsurgent violence. According
to the Chechen Interior Ministry, between the end of
April and November, 118 combatants died. Of the incidents,
we should highlight one operation by the Chechen security forces in mid-November, with an official count of 20 rebels killed. In parallel, the

North Caucasus insurgency claimed responsibility for an attack on a luxury train 320 kilometers from Moscow in November, which caused 26 deaths and close to one hundred wounded, although several analysts had doubts about their participation. In addition, the counterinsurgency cooperation between Chechnya and Ingushetia increased. Meanwhile, **grave human rights violations continued**, including kidnappings and disappearances. Local and international organizations urged Russia to end the atmosphere of abuses against civilians. During the year several people with links to the fi elds of human rights, journalism and humanitarian work were killed,

including the activist from the NGO Memorial Natalia
Estemirova.51 In addition, in March the former Vostok
battalion commander and main rival of the Chechen
president, Sulim Yamadayev, was killed in Dubai.

Russia (Ingushetia)

Start: 2008
Type: System
Internal
Main parties: Russian Federal Government, Government of Ingushetia, armed opposition groups (Jamaat Ingush)
Intensity: 1
Trend: ?

51. See Chapter 5 (Human Rights and Transitional Justice).

Armed Conflicts **45**

out the year. There were massive arrests of activists and
DTP members were accused of having links with the

PKK after the March elections, in which the DTP won by a wide margin in the southeast. Protests were launched in response to the arrests and caused the death of at least one police officer and dozens of wounded. Tension increased significantly in December for two reasons: an attack by a PKK cell in the province of Tokat (centre) without orders from above which caused the death of seven soldiers and had a considerable political and social impact; and because of a judicial order to ban the DTP, accused of cooperating with the PKK. **The latter considered the position of the Government and the State an attempt to wipe out the group and its bases**; criticized the new conditions of Öcalan's arrest; and threatened with a

process of no return in reference to a renewal of violence. Subsequent Kurdish demonstrations
in numerous cities resulted in three civilians dead and several wounded. Massive arrests at the end of the year against Kurdish circles, including mayors from the DTP, resulted in 300 accused.

Middle East

Iraq
Start: 2003
Type: System, Government, Resources
Internationalized internal
Main parties: Transitional Government, international
coalition led by the USA/ United Kingdom, internal and external armed opposition groups
Intensity: 3
Trend: =
Summary:
The invasion by the US-led coalition in March 2003, based
on the alleged existence of weapons of mass

destruction as a justification and with the purpose of overthrowing Saddam Hussein's regime on the grounds of supposed links to the attacks of September 11, 2001 in New York, gave rise to the beginning of an armed conflict that has gradually involved an increasing number of actors: international troops, Iraqi Armed Forces, militias and insurgent groups and al-Qaeda, among others. The new power-sharing arrangement between Sunnis, Shiites and Kurds within the constitutional framework introduced following Hussein's overthrow has aroused discontent in many sectors. Violence has been on the rise and armed opposition to the international presence in the country has given way to an internal power struggle with a strong sectarian bent since February 2006, mainly between Shiites and Sunnis.

The country continued to undergo high levels of violence which intensifi ed in the second quarter with the withdrawal of US troops from Iraqi cities in June and with the approach of the elections planned for the beginning of 2010 (the second general election since Saddam Hussein was ousted). The continuous attacks, suicide

Turkey (Southeast)
Start: 1984
Type: Self-government, Identity
Internationalized internal
Main parties: Government, PKK, TAK
Intensity: 2
Trend: ⍰
Summary:
The PKK, founded in 1978 as a Marxist-Leninist political

party led by Abdullah Öcalan, announced an armed offensive in 1984 against the Government and launched a military insurgency campaign to demand Kurdistan's independence. This prompted a strong response from the Government in defence of territorial integrity. The resulting war between the PKK and the Government particularly affected the Kurdish civilian population in south-eastern Turkey, trapped in the crossfire and victim of persecutions and forcible evacuation campaigns carried out by the Government. The conflict took a new turn in 1999, with the arrest of Öcalan and the subsequent announcement by the PKK that it was abandoning the armed struggle and transforming its goals. It would cease in its demands for independence to focus on fighting for the recognition

of the Kurdish identity within Turkey. With Turkey's
anti-terrorist discourse and the PKK claiming a policy of selfdefence,
the conflict remained alive as a socio-political crisis
in subsequent years and escalated in 2007. **An opportunity for peace during the year, as a result of
the trust building measures by the Government and the
PKK, was jeopardized at the end of the year with the
banning of the pro-Kurdish party DTP and an upturn in
violence.** Until November fighting had declined considerably,
although there were several clashes and crossborder
operations by the Army against the PKK, with dozens of deaths. According to the group, 128 soldiers
and 94 combatants died during 2009. The PKK, which

had formally maintained a non-offensive position since the end of 2008 until the local elections in March 2009, announced **a new ceasefire in April. The PKK subsequently renewed it** and simultaneously made calls for dialogue and its leader, Abdullah Öcalan52 requested the creation of a road map. **The Government, in an about-face regarding its earlier position, announced in July the preparation of reforms to resolve the Kurdish question** which it presented to the Parliament in November. The plan was rejected by the opposition and supported by the Army, who was determined to finish off the PKK. In this sense, the Parliament renewed for

another year the Army's permission to attack the group
in Iraq. This decision was considered by the PKK to be
a declaration of war. Moreover, the armed group considered
the Government's reform plan ambiguous. Even so,
the PKK sent, at the initiative of Öcalan and as a peace
gesture, a group of 34 people –eight combatants and
24 civilian refugees– from Iraq to Turkey in October.
However, the mass reception they were offered in
Diyarbakir was harshly criticized by the Turkish political
class. Furthermore, the tension between the State and
Kurdish social and political sectors was visible through-

52. See Chapter 3 (Peace processes).

An opportunity for

peace was created with trust building measures by the PKK and the Government, although in December violence was on the rise and the DTP Kurdish party was banned

46 Alert 2010

president Barack Obama. He had anticipated the departure of combat troops in August 2010 with 50,000 troops remaining for limited missions until the end of 2011. Finally, just before the deadline and under pressure from the US, the Iraqi Parliament passed the voting law and the elections were scheduled for March 7. A day later the country saw one of its bloodiest days, with a

series of attacks in Baghdad that caused over one hundred
deaths. Political tension and violence also marked
the local elections in 14 of the 18 provinces in the
country at the beginning of the year and in the elections
in the Iraqi Kurdistan in July. Confl ict in the province of
Nineveh and its capital, Mosul, as well as an uncertain
political situation in the Northern oil-rich city of Kirkuk,
marked by ethnic divisions, made these areas the main
spotlight of attention due to their potential instability.
attacks and episodes of sectarian violence ended the
lives of thousands of people throughout the year. According
to a study by the organization Iraq Body Count, a total of 4,500 civilians died in 2009, half the

number of the previous year and the lowest number of civilian victims since the invasion of the country in 2003. Nevertheless, in 2009 the number of victims in large scale attacks increased. In October, the deadliest attack since 2007 killed 150 people in the centre of Baghdad, in theory one of the most heavily guarded places in the country, and which had been the scene of another attack two months earlier resulting in over one hundred dead. Towards the end of the year the situation of insecurity and the diffi culties in passing the election law which should govern the general elections raised doubts about whether the US would be able to fulfi l the **calendar of troop withdrawals announced in February**

by US

53. Tomàs, Núria, Villellas, Ana. *The Autonomous Kurdistan Region: Risks and Challenges for Peace*. Quadern de Construcció de Pau nº. 8, Escola de Cultura de Pau (School for a Culture of Peace), July 2009.
http://escolapau.uab.cat/img/qcp/kurdistan_risks_peace.pdf

Box 1.3. **Increased conflict in the "disputed territories" in Northern Iraq**

The "disputed territories" refer to a strip of land which extends from Syria to Iran along the southern edge of the Kurdistan Autonomous Region (Iraq). Once the stage for the Arabization policy of Saddam Hussein's regime, followed by the expulsion of the Kurdish population, the situation in these areas constitutes the principle axis of growing tension between the Kurdish government and the central powers in Baghdad. While the Kurdish authorities insist that the status of these zones be defined within the framework of the 2005 Constitution, a number of factors have made this impossible up till now, without any prospect of it taking place.53

According to the KRG, these areas include territories under the administration of Kirkuk, Nineveh (Mosul), Diyala and Wasit (Kut) and they are considered "disputed" because their internal frontiers, administrative bodies, resources and population were subjected to changes under the Arabization programs adopted decades ago by the central government. According to the KRG, these changes led to a decrease in the Kurdish population of each region, created new entities and transferred Kurdish and Turkoman land to Arab colonists. For this reason the KRG insists on looking at these policies again to define the status of these territories and, to this end, in 2003 the Kurdish authorities initiated a campaign to settle the question. On the other hand, central government is reticent about Kurdish claims and says the areas are only described as "disputed" because the

Kurds claim them.

Matters have evolved on two levels. In the legislative sphere, various articles relating to the "disputed territories" have been approved. Among the most notable is Article 58 of the 2004 Transitional Administration Law, which was later absorbed into
Article 140 of the Iraqi Constitution approved in 2005, which lays out, with some ambiguity, three phases in order to arrive
at a definitive status for these zones: "normalization", carrying out a census and holding a referendum. On the ground, various experts say that the area has progressively come under the control of the KRG, although it remains de jure under the central government. In practice, and among other measures, what this means is that there are peshmergas, Kurdish regional forces, present. As for the proposed phases, although the cut-off date for a referendum set out in the Constitution (31 December
2007) has passed, parts of the other phases have been carried out. According to the Kurdish

government, the normalization phase is complete and logistically everything is ready to carry out the census. However, the lack of agreements between the sides has blocked advances towards the holding of a referendum.

Two principal factors, each given different weight, depending on the point of view, stand out among the causes of the dispute. On the one hand, the difficult area of the "disputed territories" is presented as a question of dignity and historical justice, rooting the problem in the policy adopted for decades by the Baghdad government. On the other hand, others see the existence of oil as the main factor in the dispute. According to the first point of view, there must be reparations for the damage suffered in the past, and to this end they see the application of Article 140 as the only and perfect solution. According the second analysis, oil is the fundamental factor in the dispute, linked to the perceived aspirations towards independence and the centrifugal forces around of Erbil. In parallel to an increase in political tension, an increase in direct violence in the "disputed territories" has been identified: violence has taken place in various ways, with continuous bomb attacks that have left dozens of deaths, and also killings and numerous incidents. The two main troubled areas are located in the areas of Mosul and Kirkuk. Near the latter, a large-scale attack in mid-June left a death toll of more than 70 and wounded nearly 200 people.

It should be borne in mind that the violence in the "disputed territories", which manifests itself in many ways and is in itself complex and multidimensional, sometimes becomes extremely diffused. According to some analysts, there is a perception that "everyone and no one" is behind the violence. Even so, various factors that contribute to violence in the "disputed territories"

rebuild what had been destroyed during the Israeli

operation in December and January.55 In September, an extensive report commissioned by the UN and led by the South African judge Richard Goldstone denounced the **commission of crimes of war during the Gaza conflict**. It accused Israel of using disproportionate force and indiscriminate attacks against civilians; and Hamas of launching missiles against Israeli territory. The text, which was passed by the UN Human Rights Commission and sparked a heated controversy, recommends sending the case to the International Criminal Court if the parties do not adequately investigate the allegations of abuses.56 In the political sphere, the February elections in Israel brought to power the Likud in coalition with the extreme right parties. Expectations regarding the new US administration's plan to advance the peace process tailed off during the year in the face of **Washington's difficulty in getting a commitment from Benjamin Netanyahu's Government to halt the construction of settlements in the West Bank and East Jerusalem**, a condition that the Palestinians consider indispensable.57 In December, the Israeli Government showed its willingness to suspend for ten months the construction of colonies in the West Bank, but it maintained its policy of demolishing Palestinian homes and announced the construction of another 700 homes in East Jerusalem.

At the end of the year, the death of an Israeli and six
Palestinians during incidents in the West Bank and
Gaza provoked fears about a new increase of violence.

Yemen
Start: 2004
Type: System
Internal
Main parties: Government, followers of the cleric
al-Houthi (al-Shabab al-Mumen)
Intensity: 2
Trend: ⚠

Israel – Palestine
Start: 2000
Type: Self-government, Identity, Territory
Internacional54
Main parties: Israeli government, colonist militias,
PNA, Fatah (Al Aqsa Martyrs Brigades), Hamas (Ezzedin al Qassam Brigades), Islamic Jihad, FPLP, FDLP, Popular

Resistance Committees
Intensity: 2
Trend: ?
Summary:
The conflict between Israel and the different Palestinian actors is renewed in 2000 with the outbreak of the second Intifada caused by the failure of the peace process initiated at the beginning of the 1990s (Oslo Process, 1993-1994). The Israeli-Palestinian conflict dates back to 1947 when UN Security Council Resolution 181 divided the territory of Palestine, then under British mandate, into two states. Shortly afterwards the State of Israel was proclaimed (1948). A Palestinian state has yet to materialise. In 1948, Israel annexed West Jerusalem, while Egypt and Jordan occupied Gaza and

the West Bank respectively. In 1967, Israel invaded East Jerusalem, the West Bank and Gaza after winning the Six-Day War against the Arab countries. Autonomy for the Palestinian territories was not formally recognised until the Oslo agreements, though its implementation would be prevented by military occupation and the territorial controls imposed by Israel.

The year began with high levels of violence due to the Israeli offensive on Gaza which lasted from December 27, 2008 to January 19, 2009. The so-called Operation "Cast Lead" concluded with 1,400 Palestinians dead –half of them civilians– and 13 Israeli victims –three of them civilians–. Although the air and land campaigns

ended, during the whole year Israel maintained their
blockade of Palestinian territory, which worsened the
humanitarian crisis caused by the lack of access of the
population to basic goods, services and materials to

can be identified, although the origin of the violence is the subject of diametrically opposed points of view. For some – among them Kurdish government sources – the al-Qaeda network is the main source of the violence or, at least, them along with Baathist insurgents backed by Syria. Those who attribute the violence to outside forces also highlight the presence of violent Saudi and Yemeni elements as a key factor. Others blame neighbouring countries, such as Turkey, for supporting opposition groups.

Others, however, highlight the violence's internal origin. In this respect, analysts interviewed lay some of the responsibility at the door of the KRG, For example, the massive presence of heavily armed peshmergas in such small areas (such as the city of Kirkuk) alongside other militias (Sunni Arabs and Turkomans) – although on a much smaller scale – has inflamed the situation. To this must be added the aggressive statements made by all sides. Some sources consulted also consider that maintaining a level of violence in the area is in Kurdish leaders' interest, adding that there is a developing power struggle between the PUK and the KDP. Central government has also made aggressive moves, such as the sending of tanks to Khanaqin in 2008. At the same time, the tight control maintained by the Iraqi National Police in Mosul significantly inflames the situation.

There is evidently a risk of escalating conflict. To avoid it, it would help if the recent rhetoric were toned down, consensus was found and confidence-building and peacebuilding policies were initiated urgently.

54. Although " Palestine" (whose Palestine

National Authority is a political entity linked to a specific population and territory) is not an internationally
recognized State, the conflict between Israel and Palestine is considered "international" and not "internal" since it is a territory which has been illegally occupied and it is not recognized as being part of Israel under International Law or by a United Nations resolution.

55. See Chapter 4 (Humanitarian crises).
56. See Chapter 5 (Human Rights and Transitional Justice).
57. See Chapter 3 (Peace processes).

48 Alert 2010

58. See Chapter 4 (Humanitarian crises).
59. See Foreign Policy. *The Failed States Index 2009*. Washington DC: Foreign Policy, 2009, in <http://www.foreignpolicy.com/articles/2009/06/22/2009_failed_states_index_interactive_map_and_rankings>.

Summary:
This conflict began in 2004, when followers of the cleric al-Houthi, who belonged to the Shiite minority,

began an uprising in the north of Yemen with the aim of reinstating a theocratic regime similar to the one that disappeared in 1962. The rebels have always accused the government of corruption and of failing to pay attention to the northern mountainous regions of the country, while objecting to its alliance with the US in the fight against terrorism. The conflict has caused the death of thousands of people and the displacement of thousands more. Violence increased at the beginning of 2007 until a peace agreement was reached in June of that year. However, sporadic fighting and accusations of breaking the agreement continued.

Violence increased signifi cantly in Yemen as part of the conflict between the Government and the followers of al-Houthi, in the north of the country, having a dramatic impact on the civilian population. In the first quarter, mutual accusations were repeated of noncompliance with the ceasefire agreed to in 2008. Beginning in August, fighting increased after the **Government launched a widespread offensive, called Operation Scorched Earth, against the Shiite insurgents.** The clashes forced the displacement of 75,000 people which makes a total of 175,000 since hostilities began in 2004. Humanitarian agencies and NGOs point to the grave situation of the civilian population which is often trapped in combat zones.58 In September, it was reported the death of 87 people in a refugee camp, allegedly caused by the security forces. Restricted access to the area of conflict made humanitarian aid and independent verification of the number of victims difficult. According to estimates there could be as many as one hundred victims including civilians and combatants.

In the last quarter the conflict threatened to escalate into a regional problem due to the growing involvement of Saudi Arabia and Iran. At the same time, Yemen faced two other sources of conflict. The first was located in the south of the country, where recurring demonstration were taking place to denounce governmental discrimination towards the region and clashes between pro-independence groups and security forces which resulted in twenty deaths. The second source of conflict had to do with al-Qaeda since the Yemeni and Saudi branches announced their integration in January. During the year clashes between the Yemeni security forces and alleged members of al-Qaeda caused the death of at least fifty people and another six were sentenced to death for collaborating with the network. At the end of 2009, international attention was focused on Yemen because of a failed attack on an airplane in route to the US. The young Nigerian attacker had been trained in Yemeni territory. Al-Qaeda in the Arabian Peninsula claimed responsibility for the action and

claimed it was a retaliation for the offensive by the
Yemeni forces with support from the US that caused the
death of at least 60 of its members.

Box 1.4. Destabilization factors in Yemen

On May 22, 2010 Yemen will celebrate its 20th anniversary as a State after unification in 1990 of the Yemen Arab Republic (YAR), in the north, and the People's Democratic Republic of Yemen (PDRY), in the south. The 20th anniversary of the sole Republic in the Arabian Peninsula will be celebrated in an extremely unstable context, amidst growing conflicts in the northern area of the country, with the forced displacement of thousands of people, and warnings from analysts regarding the possibility that Yemen may end up on the list of failed states. In its most recent ranking on this issue, Foreign Policy magazine placed it in a situation of high "danger" – number 18 on the list after North Korea– and warned of the possibility that it could become the next Afghanistan.59 In December 2009, after the failed attempt by a young Nigerian trained in Yemen to commit a terrorist attack on an airplane flying to Detroit, all international attention was focused on the risks the country posed as a potential haven for al-Qaeda bases. US President Barack Obama himself had warned about this possibility a few months earlier. What factors contribute to the instability of this country? What are the key elements needed to understand the conflicts that affect Yemen? Without pretending to be exhaustive, we cite below the main sources of tension and some economic, political and demographic features and trends that affect the current situation.

First, it should be pointed out that episodes of violence in the country have revolved around three areas. The main centre of conflict –practically ignored by the international community in recent years, although much more visible in 2009–, is in the north of the country where the government

forces and insurgents known as al-Houthists – followers of al-Houthi–, are fighting
in the context of the hostilities that began in 2004. The Sanaa administration accuses the rebels of attempting to restore an
imamate like the one that ruled in the area for one thousand years until the victory of the Republican revolution in 1962. That
is, a clerical regime following the principles of Zaidism –a minority branch of Shiism in Yemen, but which holds the majority
in the north of the country–. The al-Houthists, therefore, accuse the Government of corruption and marginalizing the north of
the country. They have condemned Sanaa's alliance with the US in its campaign against terrorism. The conflict has taken
place against a background of sectarian identities, regional underdevelopment and a perception of historical injustice. It has
caused hundreds of deaths between the civilian population and combatants as well as a severe humanitarian crisis in the area
due to the forced displacement of 175,000

people. Restricted access to the region has made it impossible to conduct an external evaluation of the conflict and of reports that cite the use of unconventional weapons and the recruitment of children and Ethiopians and Somalis for combat. At the end of 2009 international concern focused on the possibility that the conflict could intensify due to the intervention of neighbouring countries and even trigger a regional escalation. Saudi Arabia inter

60. See Human Rights Watch. *In the Name of Unity: The Yemeni Government's Brutal Response to Southern Movement Protests*. Washington DC, HRW, 15 December 2009, in <http://www.hrw.org/en/reports/2009/12/15/name-unity-0>

61. See Phillips, Sarah and Shanahan, Rodger. *Al Qaida, Tribes and Instability in Yemen*. Sydney: Lowy Institute for International Policy, November 2009, in

<http://www.humansecuritygateway.com/documents/LOWY_AlQaida_Tribes_Instability_Yemen.pdf> and Bakier, Abdul Hamed. "Al-Qaeda in Yemen Supports Southern Secession". *Terrorism Monitor*, Vol. VII, 16, (June 12, 2009), in <http://www.jamestown.org/uploads/media/TM_007_32.pdf>.

62. In August, al-Qaeda in the Arabian Peninsula launched an unsuccessful terrorist attack against the Saudi prince Mohammed bin Nayef, who is responsible for Saudi anti-terrorist activities, with the same kind of explosive used by the young Nigerian in the failed attack on a flight between Amsterdam and Detroit.

63. For more information, see Bouceck, Christopher. *Yemen: Avoiding a Downward Spiral*, Washington DC: Carnegie Endowment for International Peace, September 2009, in http://www.carnegieendowment.org/files/yemen_downward_spiral.pdf. International Crisis

Group. *Yemen: Defusing the Saada Time Bomb*. Middle East Report Nº86, Brussels: ICG, May 27, 2009, in <http://www.crisisgroup.org/home/index.cfm?id=6113&l=1>.

vened directly against the al-Houthists in the border region beginning in November and, together with Yemen —in both countries the majority is Sunni—, have insinuated that Iran —with its Shiite majority— is backing the insurgents. Tehran denied the support and criticized the Saudi intervention. In this context, some analysts feel that if Iran was not yet giving support to the rebels they may begin considering this option due to the growing participation by Riyadh in the conflict.

In parallel, the central Yemeni Government is facing a growing secessionist movement in the south of the country, in the region which corresponds to the former PDRY which went through a period of Socialism in the 1970s and 1980s. Since the unification, the balance of power has leaned toward the north and, in fact, President Ali Abdullah Saleh (leader in the former YAR since 1978) has governed continuously since then. The fragile political balance set up when the new State was created only lasted a few years and resulted in the outbreak of a civil war in 1994 with the forces in the north eventually claiming the victory. Tension continues and during this last year there have been many demonstrations to denounce discrimination of the south, especially regarding the control of resources, and there have also been clashes with the security forces that have caused dozens of deaths. In this scenario, Human Rights Watch has warned of the climate caused by the repression of the separatist movement by the Government and of the violence that could break out in the region.60 The third source of conflict in the country—and the one which is garnering the most international attention– is linked to actions by al-Qaeda which announced the integration of its Yemeni and Saudi branches in

January. Yemen, Osama bin Laden's father's homeland, is located in a highly strategic area —where the Arabian Peninsula and the Horn of Africa meet— with porous borders and areas of their territory that escape government control. These factors make the territory an ideal base for al-Qaeda activity; even more so given that the Yemeni security forces have focused their attention on the conflicts that affect the north and south of the country and that Yemen seems to be a more viable refuge because pursuit of its members has increased in neighbouring Saudi Arabia. What is now called al-Qaeda in the Arabian Peninsula, which is currently led by the former private secretary of bin Laden, Nasir al-Wuhayshi, has been operating in the country for years, especially against Western interests (17 marines died in 2000 in a terrorist attack against the U.S. Navy destroyer USS Cole and another 19 people died in an attack against the US embassy in Sanaa in 2008). According to some analysts, the group could strengthen its positions in Yemen by establishing relations with local tribes and exploiting the conflicts that affect the country, for example, by expressing support for the secessionist struggle in the south as it did in mid-2009.61 Even before the failed terrorist attack in Detroit, the US had intensified its collaboration with Yemeni forces in its battle against al-Qaeda, considering that the group had shown signs that it was looking for higher profile targets in its attacks. It was also believed that this branch could attempt to get stronger considering the pressure the bin Laden network was under in Afghanistan and Pakistan.62

Along with these three sources of conflict, Yemen faces another series of challenges that also threaten its political future. These include social, economic and demographic problems that could heighten the climate of destabilization. In the economic sphere, we should note that it is the poorest country in the Arab world and has high rates of unemployment and inflation, as well as significant levels of corruption. In addition, most of the State's resources –around 75%– come from oil revenues and the reserves are rapidly being depleted. Some estimations state that these resources will not last more than five years while other more optimistic forecasts place the limit in 2017. These reserves are not the only ones that are in jeopardy in Yemen. Alarms have been raised regarding the dramatic decrease in the country's water supplies, placing it among the nations with the greatest water shortages in the world, according to the United Nations. The situation looks even more complex if we consider that these economic factors must be understood in the framework of a rising demographic trend: the Yemeni population is expected to double to 40 million people in the next twenty years. Currently, over two thirds of the population is below age 24, and the predictions are that in coming years a growing and impoverished population could increase its pressure on the Government that traditionally has had problems exercising central power. In Yemen tribal dynamics continue to play an important role and the population is heavily armed despite efforts by the Government to control the extensive use of light arms in most of the cities in the country. Given the situation, specialized analysts have alerted to the need for both local actors and the international community to act quickly to avoid a worsening of violence in Yemen and they remind us that although the country has overcome several crises and situations of instability in the past, it has never had to face a combination of challenges so complex to resolve.63